This book is affectionately
dedicated to the people of
St. Chad, Erdington

Once God has spoken;
twice have I heard this;
that power belongs to God;
and that to thee, O Lord, belongs
steadfast love.

Ps 62:11–12

POWER
TO THE
POWERLESS
Theology Brought to Life

Laurie Green

Introduction by David Sheppard

Marshall Pickering

261

Marshall Morgan and Scott
Marshall Pickering
3 Beggerwood Lane, Basingstoke, Hants RG23 7LP, UK

Copyright © 1987 Laurie Green
First published in 1987 by Marshall Morgan and Scott
Publications Ltd
Part of the Marshall Pickering Holdings Group
A subsidiary of the Zondervan Corporation

ISBN 0 551 01570 1   20014475

Phototypeset in Linotron Ehrhardt
by Input Typesetting Ltd, London

Printed in Great Britain by
Guernsey Press Ltd, Guernsey C.I.

Contents

Acknowledgments

Most of all I would like to thank all those people of St. Chad's church, many of whom appear in this book, who gave so freely of themselves to make our visions of a grass-roots theology into a reality. Most of our meetings were tape-recorded and transcribed so that quotations which appear in this text are authentic, save for the fact that I felt it necessary here and there to disguise the source of more confidential and personal contributions. The book only gives the bare outline of an extensive and complex process which was tremendously demanding of all concerned. In the background were two friends who acted as encouragers and who also supervised the doctoral work in which I was simultaneously engaged. They are the Revd. Dr. John J. Vincent, Director of the Urban Theology Unit in Sheffield and the Revd. Dr. Dick Snyder of New York Theological Seminary. I owe to them both a great debt of gratitude for their friendship and advice.

I also want to thank Madeleine Levasseur and Pat Fletcher for their willingness to transform my handwritten scripts into neat type and to Jeni Parsons for her careful critique of my first draft. Amongst those who encouraged me along the way, I thank especially my close friends Mother Frances Dominica and the Revd. Robin Morrison. And finally, I simply want to ask Vicki, Rebecca and Hannah how they put up with me constantly skiving off to write another page when it was my turn to do the washing up!

My love and thanks to all.

Laurie

Introduction

In recent years Christians in Britain have become aware of Urban Priority Areas as never before. There has been much talk about local leadership, about releasing God-given intelligence, about the growth of personal confidence which has been repeatedly trampled on, and about local, urban theology. Many Christians who associate theology with libraries and colleges and ancient texts wonder what this talk is about. Many find the emphasis on urban priority areas disturbing and even subversive. Laurie Green's account of a small group of urban Christians holding together their experience in Birmingham and the parables and life of the Gospels spells out how urban theology can transform daily living. It rings bells for me with my own experiences of Urban Priority Areas in Liverpool and London. It will, I believe, bring new hope and stimulus to many in such areas. For those whose life keeps them hurrying up and down the motorway of successful, comfortable Britain, this story of what happened in a parish in the shadow of Spaghetti Junction offers honest insight into urban life and a vivid chance to learn from Urban Priority Area Christians. I hope many others will be encouraged to pull off the Motorway and listen to what may be learned from 'under the motorway'. This book will call in question some of the models of success which may be held up in better-attended Churches. It has, I believe, searching and stimulating lessons from which all Christians could learn.

At heart it is so simple – and could happen in any area. Gather a group of local people together. Let them tell and share their stories of their own personal lives and their experiences of the community in which they live. It takes time for the group to gather confidence and trust in each other. Soon questions begin to form. When was that road built, what stood there before, how did that happen, why have people in the area been robbed of making choices, if they have to spend great proportions of their time waiting how can Christ come into that experience? The questions precede the search for more information, for clearer analysis. The group becomes energised. There's enthusiasm, there's co-oper-ation. One promises to take on a particular task if another will support her. Soon a clear profile of an area is written.

The group moves to the Bible. One parable or story after another is worked through. New connections are made, new questions asked. Eyes and ears are opened. The theme emerges of Parables in Action. Action grows naturally from the study.

The 'Parables in Action' group at St Chad's opened an advice Centre. They worked to raise the money. They became the Advice Centre workers. People came. Needs were met. In the thick of it workers became keenly aware of Christ's presence.

Most had started off saying we can't do it, we don't know enough. Now they discovered new Christian resources in Scripture, in community action, in themselves. They discovered the ancient Christian experience, that the Word was made flesh and dwelt among us.

Laurie Green's book is important because it spells out a story of a small pilgrim people who discovered new sources of 'love in action'. It is within reach of Christian groups in every part of the country. I believe it will be a very useful tool especially in emerging groups in urban priority areas.

David Sheppard,
Bishop of Liverpool,
June 1987.

1: To Make Theology Democratic

A. Catching up with God's world

We live in an exciting and challenging age. The pages of history seem to be turning faster in our generation than anyone has ever experienced before. We add to our vast store of knowledge by the hour; we are introduced to crises and problems at every news broadcast. We are horrified one moment, we are elated the next, by the flood of information that flows our way; we are amused, confronted or controlled at every turn. What an exciting and exhilarating era in which Christians are expected to respond, contribute and initiate.

Here in Britain, I am constantly meeting people, ordinary committed Christians, who are so excited by the challenges of our times and by the vitality of their faith that they are straining at the leash to find ways of responding to the situation with integrity, justice and compassion. They are searching, yearning indeed, for faith which is related to God's concern for peace, justice and mutual respect in His world, but they sometimes despair at the meagre resources of Christian understanding with which they have been equipped for the task. Even those who have undertaken courses of theological study complain that their real problem remains – of making the relevant connections between that theological study and what is now happening in the life of the world around them. Not everyone has had the opportunity of a theological education of course, but most Christians will have had a chance to attend Bible studies, Lent courses and the like, put on by the local parish church. But, as every parish priest knows, the problem still remains of making the vibrant connections between what is being studied and the fast-

changing challenges of the world about us. And the more we
manage to feel the urgency of what is happening in God's
world, the more we feel the vital necessity of making connections between that world and all the wonderful treasures of
our Christian tradition and faith, for it is only by making
those connections that we can begin to see the Christian
meaning and significance of what is happening all around
us.

Being alive to those meanings and significances is a fine
aim to which Christians aspire but most ordinary church-
going people will say, 'I just don't have the theology to make
sense of this modern situation; my faith seems unrelated to
life's issues.' Some others who have heard about the exciting
developments in this field in other lands will observe: 'I've
heard about liberation theology in other countries, but what
can we do here?' Others who have perhaps been offered
Christian 'answers' to life's problems may feel that full justice
has not been done by the Church to the depth and complexity
of the issues. The answers seem too slick for their taste and
they complain, 'They're wallpapering over the great cracks
in our society with a lovely flouncy wallpaper of religiosity
which will only rip to pieces when the wall crumbles'.

Thus, it is from many quarters that we hear this frustration
and dissatisfaction amongst those who want to find ways of
bringing life's issues together with the Christian faith
tradition in a lively and active way so that something exciting
and productive may ensue.

However, we should not be content only to paint this bleak
picture, for I also come across folk who have been lucky
enough to hear of some of the exciting experiments up and
down our own country where groups of Christians have
found ways of bringing God's concern for the world right
into the heart of their faith. It has brought those groups
alive in an extraordinary way. They have certainly not shut
themselves off from the horrors of the injustices of our
society, indeed they are immersed in those realities, and
yet they have found their faith in the risen Lord inspiring,
invigorating and challenging them to create new ways of
witnessing to his presence in the suffering world. Often, they
are small groups clustering around a common concern about

which they are convinced God has something to say and some action to demand of them. Many will be found in the churches of our inner cities and council estates, some will be at work places or unemployment centres or in the blighted rural communities. They spring up like luxuriant poppies in a field of burnt stubble.

This little book is an attempt to share the experiences of just one such experiment where ordinary Christians gathered together over a period of years in a small back-street church in Birmingham and together hammered out a faith and theology by which they felt they could live and die. They had to immerse themselves in the world and really face up to the issues which confronted them on the Birmingham streets. From their reflections upon their situation they began to build many insights which came to them from the Bible and from the traditions of our faith.

But as this book will recount, the story was not to end simply in talk and reflection, for their newly-learnt awareness of what was under the skin of society led to some very exciting and challenging community action. The group's theological analysis inspired them to set up an advice centre run *for* the people and *by* the people of that inner city community. No sooner had they begun that mammoth undertaking, than they found themselves reflecting once again on all that their new experience was teaching them. From this constant interplay of action and reflection grew up a fascinating theology which was not imposed from outside the situation but which was generated by God's activity alongside His people in that place.

But before any reader gets the false impression that all this came about without a struggle, let me say immediately that the experience of this Birmingham group, of which I was myself a member, only goes to prove how difficult a task it is for Christians today to make these vital connections between our modern situation and the keynotes of our faith. Time and again, we found obstacles in our path. Repeatedly we found that something within us held us back from looking honestly at our society or hearing clearly the tough questions which were coming at us from the Bible. It was as if we had been shielded by our upbringing from looking too deeply at

the realities and had been taught unconsciously over the
years to be accepting of all that was around us and not to
hold it up to the fierce light of the Gospel critique. We had
even learnt to read the Gospel in a very watered-down way
and the tough things Jesus had to say to us had long been
dissolved in a sugary mixture which saved us from responding
at all courageously. Not content to blame our upbringing
alone, we became aware of our own deep inner preference
for holding fast to the anchors of the old prejudices and
stereotypes about the world around us and about Jesus'
message rather than to be turned upside down by what God
was in fact doing and saying. We found ourselves preferring
the security of our prejudices rather than the excitement and
risk of the Gospel of Jesus.

B. Where our feet are, there shall our hearts be also

In order to get started, let us take a moment to look at how
it is that we can be blinkered from the Gospel's challenge
by the society in which we live. To do this, we need to
remind ourselves of the tremendous influence which our own
place in society, our 'incarnation' if you like, has in how we
perceive and understand the fast moving world that
surrounds us.

We begin by registering the obvious fact that the way we
decide to contribute to our society will be greatly influenced
by how we perceive what is happening within it. And how
we perceive things will in turn be largely determined by
where we are situated within that society. In other words, we
might say 'where our feet are, there shall our hearts be also'.
If I am a reasonably well-heeled suburban white, then what
I will see of my society may well lead me to become a secure
and reliable citizen who works hard to see the values of my
society flourish and function smoothly. Conversely, if I am a
poor white or an urban black in the same society, my experience may be so bad that my interpretation of that society
leads me to campaign or rebel against it in whatever way
comes to hand. Thus, my response to society will largely be

decided by the place I myself have in that society – the place from which I experience it.

Having however reflected for a moment upon how important the place and position of our 'incarnation' might be, we must, on the other hand, stress that we human beings are not entirely determined by our situation. We have some liberty to make our own responses. Given that the situation into which we are born must be very influential in determining our choices, we nevertheless can respond in a variety of ways. Everyone knows that even brothers and sisters of the same family will be individuals and will take different paths to adulthood. But the problem remains that the number of choices one has will always be very largely determined by the opportunities offered by one's environment and place in society. So a doctor's son in Surrey will have, to say the least, rather more choices than a factory cleaner's daughter in Newcastle! But it will always be strangely difficult to admit to this obvious fact for deeply engrained within the British mind is a weighty conservatism and reluctance to be actively critical of the dominant ideas of our own society. We may gently 'knock' the British way of doing things from time to time, but scratch any of us too deeply, or allow a foreigner to criticise our ways, and it's altogether a different story. We simply do not feel it right seriously to criticise our society at its roots, preferring to complain only about the symptoms of its malaise. It seems that one of the disadvantages of having 'won' two world wars is that our apparent success reinforced the belief in 'the way things are with us'. Other 'defeated' nations had heavily to criticise their structures and ideals, and hence, were forced to question aspects of themselves of which they would otherwise have remained proud.

Within the British people there seems to be a lingering spirit, longing for those questionable pre-war attributes of dependency, privilege and patronage; qualities which perhaps should have been rethought rather than reinforced. Instead of this, we have been taught to play our part over so many generations in maintaining the accepted systems without too much question. Our educational institutions are increasingly directed by governments not to 'educate thinkers' who may in their wisdom question the *status quo* but to concentrate

on 'vocational training' which is supposed to guide pupils
smoothly into jobs which will fulfil the need of the structure
of society, keeping it running without rocking the boat. Even
the Church institution is asked to play its part in maintaining
this unchallenged acceptance of the *status quo* and is expected
to give its blessing to every arm of the state and establishment.
If ever our Gospel demands that we speak a prophetic word
of criticism to the state, we are accused of not fulfilling our
proper 'function' of praying for and blessing on its way, the
social structure which moulds the lives of our people.

In more recent years, however, our society has become
more technologically advanced and so this maintaining aspect
of the Church's function has become less important to the
state than in former times. The advent of the technological
media of communication has overtaken religion in its ability
to reach down into the psychological depths of the people to
assist their conformity to the requirements of our particular
social and economic system. The constant repetition of
advertisements, the replaying of the adventures of the heroes
of the consumer society on every television screen, help to
inculcate into the people all the necessary ways of thinking,
feeling and wanting which tend to keep this particular social
system intact[1]. Even when problems do flare up into the
public consciousness, the news broadcasts stress the excitement and exhilaration of trouble, and treating the issues in
'Hollywood' style, rarely investigate the underlying nature of
the social malaise. As a consequence, it proves very difficult,
and calls for a great deal of creative imagination to become
conscious of the things that are truly wrong in our society.
It is as if we as a society are reluctant to become aware of
the disagreeable realities of our own failings and continually
find ways to convince ourselves that everything is all right.
However, for a large number of British people and for an
even larger proportion of the population of our world today,
life is bitter, brutal and short.[2]

So the world of human beings is harsh and at times is so
ruthlessly selfish that it blinds itself to its own shortcomings.
But it is this tough world of reality into which Jesus Christ
was born. The incarnation of Jesus does not point us to a
God who likes the soft option but to a Father intent on

addressing the tough and knotty issues of an unjust world of human strife and folly. For if our earlier maxim holds true, that where our feet are there shall our hearts be also, then we are now made to conjure with the question of why God willed that his Son should experience the poorer end of his society. For Jesus was born a political refugee in a backwater town in a land torn apart by intrigue and turmoil. He grew up speaking a minority language in Galilee, that hotbed of revolutionary activity, where the struggle against the harsh rule of the Romans was most bitterly felt and fought. During his childhood, Jesus would have experienced the destruction of the local town of Sepphoris, and the annihilation of its populace by the Romans and their lacqueys, no doubt sharing the bitter emotions of his people at such an outrage.

It is from such a context that Jesus emerges.

C. A new way of seeing

As the child Jesus grew to maturity, he entered upon his ministry, proclaiming: 'The time is fulfilled, and the kingdom of God is close at hand. Repent, and believe the gospel.'[3]

Scholars have worked hard at trying to understand precisely what these words mean, but the crux of the matter seems to be that Jesus is calling for a complete about-turn in the way we think and feel about things. The time is right for it, he says. The new pattern of things, the Kingdom of God pattern, is on for us right now. And our response must be to have a mind and heart that is so orientated to this new Kingdom perspective that we break off our conformity to the old pattern and change our lives completely: that's repentance. And as part and parcel of this turn around he calls us to belief in the Gospel or Good News.

By calling for this sort of convicted belief he makes it pretty clear that he wants no wishy-washy adherence but decisive and committed action. It's like saying, 'get acting now on the firm conviction that God's Good News can be fulfilled!' And remember that Jesus is shouting this at us from the perspective of one who knows all about the rough deal that most unfortunates get in this harsh world. He really

believes that things are now possible and our faithless turning
of a blind eye or our putting justice and love off till some
distant tomorrow just will not do.

A new Kingdom perspective then, followed up by faithful
action, is his mandate upon us as he cries 'repent and
believe!' He calls for a whole new way of seeing ourselves
and the world.

When we think of his words as applying only to our individual and personal internal life, then 'repent and believe'
can be threat enough. If we remember that Jesus intended
his words to apply to our every endeavour, *both personal and
social*, then 'repent and believe' can seem as risky a mandate
as any revolutionary political manifesto! Some Christians
argue, of course, that Jesus' words are only to be understood
as referring to individuals and not to the wider society in
which God has set us. But only those who believe God's
activity to be limited to one section of his creation can say
that Jesus' saving words and actions do not relate to every
aspect of the human predicament but merely to that part
which we normally refer to as the personal. God's healing
power is simply not that limited.

Jesus, then, seems to be calling for new thinking, new
approaches and new reflections upon how things are and
how they ought to be, both within ourselves as individuals
and within ourselves as a society. Once having acquired
this 'new mind', he calls us to act upon it faithfully and
courageously. As later chapters will explain, it was just such
an experience which prompted that little church in the Birmingham back-streets to engage in its adventurous project, for
it was out of a new way of seeing themselves and the world
around them that they began to understand more of what the
Kingdom of God demanded of them in active commitment.

D. Theology plugged in

So where does theology fit into all this? I like to tell a story
about the three people who were marooned on a deserted
island with only a tin of baked beans for company. The first
said to the others, 'I am a chemist, and I can calculate how

hot we need to make the tin in order for it to explode open'. The next said, 'I am a physicist and I can calculate the trajectory of the beans so that none shall be lost'. 'I am a theologian' said the third, 'and I can imagine that we have a tin-opener'. Such has been the irrelevance of so much of the conversation of theologians of the past. However, that need not mean that theology itself should be dispensed with! If we get theology out into the open, dust it down, oil it and inspect it, we find that we have in our hands a vital tool for the job of Christian discipleship, for with proper use it will enable us to reflect upon the world in a brand new way – from the Kingdom of God perspective – and then, if we have the guts, to act faithfully upon what we newly perceive. Theology can be an active and lively reflection upon the things of God and of his ways in the world, and it is precisely this which can bring clearer focus to the 'new mindedness' of Kingdom repentance and faithful action.

You may respond by claiming that theology has quite rightly been allowed to go rusty because it was only for the bookish academics of the past. But how is it that even in the fourth century, the desert monk Evagrius Ponticus could describe the real theologian not as an academic but as 'one whose prayers are true'? Evagrius had the flair to see that the essence of theology only comes to light when devoutly and courageously used by the committed – those who are prepared not only to read and argue but to act and pray faithfully. Put his words the other way about and we can ask the question 'How will anyone be able to pray properly if they have not very carefully reflected upon the realities of God and the real-life issues of the world'? You will know what I mean if you've ever had to endure those prayers in church which seem to pray to God about all sorts of vague generalisations, obviously issuing from the mouth of someone who hasn't looked at the real world for years! And the prayers are equally 'untheological' if they read like a newspaper editorial with scarcely a mention of anything to do with the real nature of God at all.

The sort of theology which will be described in this book takes a tough look at the world and reflects upon God's activity within it as we experience it. It then thrusts us into action alongside that God who has been discerned. Theology in these terms is what many are rediscovering daily in this twentieth century world. In Latin America, for example, they are discovering it and it is issuing in liberation theology which seems to be proving a vital force for them in the rebirth of a new faithfulness in discipleship even amidst the atrocities and obscenities of the ultra-right wing political regimes of that continent.[4] We can hardly pretend any longer that theology is strictly for doddery academics when it seems in fact to have the potential, as in Latin America, for turning the world upside down! What would happen then, we must ask ourselves, if we took up this old rusty tool called theology, cleaned it up and set it to work for us?

E. Theology by the people

In doing all this, of course, we have to guard against some ominous dangers. Firstly, we must take care that *theology is democratised*. By this, I mean that it must never again be left in the hands of a scholarly or priestly élite but must be reclaimed as an essential component of every Christian's kit-bag. In the past in Britain, lay people have been made to feel both inadequate and guilty at trespassing upon theology and have been expected to treat it as the preserve of the clergy and professional university theologians. We clergy have tried to keep it to ourselves in much the same way that we managed for centuries to keep the Bible from lay Christians by having it only in Latin. It seems to me that to put theology into the hands of the people will be very good for clergy and laity alike and will help to rid our church of its caste system of those who have 'the knowledge' and those ordinary mortals who supposedly do not. So, as Ian Fraser has it in his little book, we must set about 'Reinventing Theology as the People's Work'.[5]

Secondly, this active, prayerful reflection we call theology will demand of us all a *tremendous commitment* to studious analysis, sharp thinking and courageous action. It will not be an easy option, as we allow so much of our religion to be nowadays. It will instead require energy, time and commitment, as this Birmingham story will show. The theological task will require, as always it has, that some of our number will have to specialise, will have to slog away learning the languages of the Bible, researching the history of the early church, and so on, so that they can assist God's people in the theological enterprise.[6] But theology will now be the ordinary people's task and the specialist theologians will have to work solely as consultant assistants to those who are at the sharp end of experiencing the issues which God presents to us in His world. Some of our best professional theologians in Britain are now beginning to appreciate that their laboratory is not in the library but out there in God's world with His people. For one of the essential ingredients of any proper theology is that it should be *rooted in the experience* of the group out of which it comes – if it is not, it becomes disembodied; it becomes so many words, without guts and sinews, without relevance. We have sadly to agree that much of the theology that comes out of Britain and Europe at present is precisely of this uneventful and disembodied nature. It seems to answer questions nobody is asking and seeks to reverse God's intention to turn His word into flesh by calmly turning the flesh back into interminable words.

To sound a third warning note, it has to be stressed that every generation in every place has to *make its own theology*. It is simply not on to transpose a theology from one context and expect it to be wholly relevant to another. We cannot take the liberation theology of Latin America and plonk it down here in dear old Blighty. That would be like straining at the Ugly Sister's foot to get it to fit Cinderella's glass slipper. We are two different cultures and what fits one will not necessarily fit the other.[7] Liberation theology is born of a people's experience of poverty and oppression and if we are to be true to our Latin American brothers and sisters, we can do that only by analysing our own situation as they did theirs, prayerfully reflecting upon it as they did and out of that will come faithful action. The whole process will be a theology which is authentic to the present British experience rather than being the 'rip-off' of their theology which seems to be the order of the day right now in European theology.

So, we must get on and do our own hard work, and do our own theology here in our own land.

Many readers by now may well be saying to themselves, 'This is nothing very new. We have read elsewhere that theology must get into the process of authentic renewal. We have already heard debates about these issues that have included all the latest jargon: 'hermeneutical circles of action and reflection', 'theological conscientisation', 'dialogical pedagogy' and all the other new techniques for a practical theology.' So let me explain straight away that it is not my intention to bombard readers with jargon if I can possibly help it, nor to rehearse the arguments about theologising that can be read elsewhere. It is true that at present there are many very good occasional papers, paperbacks and talks on the theory of theologising,[8] but my abiding concern of late has been to listen to the stories of those who have actually been trying to do theology alongside ordinary folk in our British settings. The wonderful thing about Britain today is that this seems to be going on more and more and I think we will be well served to have such attempts documented for all to hear.[9] It seemed right therefore to set about telling the story of one such project in which I have been fortunate enough to be involved so that others may read and learn from our mistakes and perhaps taste something of the tremendous excitement that we experienced when we sensed that something special was happening for us.

2: Getting Our Bearings

A. Walking the streets of the parish

Let me begin by describing a little of the context out of which this project sprang. Across the centre of England sprawls one of the largest industrial and commercial conurbations in Europe. At the heart of this conurbation lies the Metropolitan District of Birmingham, England's 'Second City'. It was here that many of the early great strides were made during the Industrial Revolution and the city is riddled with canals, railways, small scale early factory buildings, back-to-back artisan housing and many other reminders of those early days. Birmingham was from the first, a beehive of small-scale diverse business concerns and, in recognition of this, became known as the 'City of a thousand trades'.[1] Later, vast new industrial complexes attracted even greater numbers of workers who were now centred mainly on the larger scale vehicle manufacturing, steel and engineering processes. The city itself, quite apart from the rest of the conurbation, now has a population of just over one million. 'The heart of the nation station' is the BBC local radio's motto, aptly reminding us that at least until recently in our modern history, Birmingham has stood geographically, industrially and economically at the heart of this manufacturing nation.

From the city centre runs the eight-lane urban motorway, the Aston Expressway, which leads north to the Gravelly Hill Motorway Interchange – commonly known as Spaghetti Junction, and you only need to take one look at it to tell why! It is the biggest motorway interchange in Europe and yet is only four miles from the city centre. In one sense Spaghetti Junction holds the key to an understanding of why the community over which it towers was ever of importance. Although the area never possessed an abundance of raw materials or natural resources, it has throughout its long history been easily accessible and was therefore from the first an important trade and route intersection. Speeding along the motorway overhead, drivers have hardly a chance to notice that below the great swirl of connecting roadways can be found an equally complex industrial canal intersection. Right alongside the canal run the local and main line railway systems and below that is still to be found the original bridging point over the old River Tame. During the first half of the last century, the high ground just north of the river became an ideal site for the building of fine old houses for Birmingham's wealthy industrialists. Besides the other advantages of the area, the land rose up here so that it put these grand houses just above the smoke line of the dirty city. By 1862, when the local railway station was opened, this southern part of Erdington, as it was called, had developed into a highly desirable area.

Today's visitor, walking out from the city centre, will cross the old river by way of a now much more substantial bridge and will look up at the soaring spectacle of Spaghetti Junction with some trepidation. But visitors will have to keep their minds on the task of crossing the roads if they want to avoid the smells and dangers of the pedestrian subways that seem to burrow off in every direction. Once over the road and away from the endless stream of traffic, the pavement begins to climb up Gravelly Hill and there we see them – those fine old houses of the early industrial gentry. But it doesn't take long to become painfully aware that these dwellings, once so grand, are now over a hundred years old, often in a state of profound disrepair and far too large to act as one-family residences for the much poorer folk who now inhabit them. Although a few still have an air of grandeur, most are now boarding houses and hostels or have been divided up into numerous smaller flats, each house with an old car or two parked up on what was once the elegant front garden.

To the right the smaller houses, built a little later for the middle-classes of the last century, are of a much more manageable size by today's standards. Even so, many have

more than one family within, and now and again we notice
a house that has been turned over to other purposes – a
day nursery for children, a house mosque for local Muslim
residents, or a multi-cultural drop-in centre. In this area
there seems to be a predominance of families who settled
here some thirty or more years ago from Jamaica, St. Kitts,
Barbados and other islands. More recently have come Pakis-
tani and Bangladeshi families and, together with older white
residents and those who have come more recently from closer
into the city centre, they have created a fascinating
community. The streets are full of activity, children and
youngsters on cycles, cars being repaired by the roadside and
neighbours swapping gossip on the doorsteps. It's clear that
there is poverty here but although at night it would not be
safe to walk alone, we sense that if it wasn't for the lack of
trees at the roadside, this street would not be too bad by
inner city standards.

Not far away, however, the visitor would stumble upon a
surprising contrast. By simply crossing over at the crossroads,
we have found ourselves in what feels like pleasant suburbia.
Here there are a few fine semi-detached houses now above
fifty years old and some even newer than that. Only another
hundred yards further on and the houses are different again!
For here we are in a council housing estate which seems to
have been long forgotten by its landlords. Many residents
have worked hard on trying to keep standards up, but nevertheless there are many broken windows, many signs of heavy
vandalism and packs of dogs roaming everywhere. Some of
the houses have been boarded up altogether, perhaps
awaiting new tenants. We can walk for quite a distance
through the estate, each road looking very much like the last.
People here are going about their business, shopping at the
little shops that are dotted about – some shops in the front-
rooms of the houses themselves. Quite a lot of the young
people, again of all races, seem to be out of work, but many
women have found part-time work. Despite a happy atmosphere there are clearly quite a lot of problems.

Turning right the visitor would at last meet the other main
road that comes off Spaghetti Junction. Across the main road
is a vast reach of industrial landscape. The three great cooling

towers of the power station and the now empty sheds and
workshops of the industrial engineers stare at us from across
the busy highway. The busyness of the commuter traffic
coming from the Junction contrasts strangely with the still-
ness of the declining industrial landscape.

Past the fish and chip shop, a grocer's shop and the garage
and up a one-way street and here the houses, although small,
are very pleasant. The road leads back towards the estate but
half-way up on the left is a building slightly set back from
the road. It's a new brick hall that has been attached to a
temporary Terrapin construction. In front is a small carpark-
cum-playground and at the roadside stands a large wooden
cross. Here, hidden away in the backstreets of the
community, we have found the church of St. Chad.

The congregation that gathers here Sunday by Sunday is
half Church of England (or Anglican) and half Methodist.
Like the community from which it is drawn, it is well mixed,
both socially and racially, and numbers approximately one
hundred and seventy, including all the children and adults. In
1974 three local Christian congregations, the two Methodist
Societies of Gravelly Hill and Bromford and the Anglican
congregation of St. Chad, covenanted together to share all
their worship and work and 'St. Chad's Ecumenical Project'
was instituted. Since then it has inevitably taken time and
care to bring the people together and establish the bond of
trust and fellowship necessary to go forward as a united
church. But St. Chad's has been remarkably blessed on its
road to unity though ecumenical projects were few and far
between in Britain when they first made the decision to
unite.[2] It is from the perspective of this small united church
set in a highly urbanised community that this story is told. I
had, at that time, been the vicar of the parish for some seven
years.

B. What we intended to do

It was soon after our congregations had become one that we
set about a major analysis of our locality and its needs and,
after bringing considerable political pressure to bear,

managed to get the local government to fund the establishment of a community centre for the area.[3] This left our church free to consider its next step as Christ's servant of the community in which he had placed us. In order to do this, we embarked upon a new phase of regular Tuesday evening workshops which began life in much the same way that many parish discussion groups or class meetings might have begun. In a back room at St. Chad's Church on October 16th 1979, a group of about a dozen rather cold people met with the very simple intention of investigating what parables are, how they operate and how the parable idea might help us in our work as a Christian group in our part of Birmingham. We had never looked specifically and thoroughly at the parables of Jesus and I wanted to invite the group to do so now, for my hope was that by returning to this bedrock of Christian tradition, we might find the right foundation on which to build our immediate future.[4] The group numbered among its members a milkman, two office workers, a press operator, a rubber tyre maker, one local primary school teacher and three housewives. Some other members were not in paid employment at that time and two were retired. I was a member of the group from its outset and my tasks were defined as the needs arose. The group was racially mixed and had a reasonable age range. It was by no means the first time we had engaged together in discussion and we felt we already knew one another pretty well but, as we gained experience, so we began to discover a distinctive style and educational approach which proved exciting and productive for us. At this stage, it's perhaps important to describe something of this style, for it played a significant part in enabling the group democratically and freely to engage in active theology.

(i) To raise up the tough questions

We wanted to find a method which would keep us open and alert, aware as we were that it's all too easy for Christians to accept, without question or discussion, what they've always been told about the meaning of the faith. We found from the outset that the only way to develop the right sort of critical consciousness was to learn the habit of asking sometimes quite simple questions together of one another and of the data. To turn a blanket statement such as 'there are poor people in the world', into a series of questions would transform the discussion overnight. To ask: 'Why are there poor people? Where are they and who are they?' put the matter onto an altogether different level. To see an issue in problem form like this, or to use the jargon, to 'problematise' it, presents the issue as a wide open problem for thought and investigation, thus disqualifying the simple imposition of ready-made definitions and clichés. We found that it was psychologically impossible to isolate something as a problem and then continue to remain detached from it as a mere spectator. Once you see an issue no longer as a statement of fact but as a problem to be solved, then you become obliged to do something about it.[5] We had therefore to begin in our group to get ourselves into the habit of being questioners and, as one of the team said some years later – 'We have developed the power here to contradict and search; we have the power here to ask *real* questions. That's what gives our thinking some real cutting edge.'

(ii) To maintain creative tension

We wanted to keep a healthy tension between the realities of the harsh world around us and the Christian hope of something very different. The way Jesus was able to look at the world, appreciate and understand it, and then to critique it from the perspective of the 'Kingdom' alternative, seems to be a way of operating theologically and faithfully which we will always have great difficulty emulating. We have to be sure not to be thoroughly subjective and pretend that the world already is the way our imagination wishes it to be. On the other hand, it is equally dangerous for us to pretend that the harsh world of facts and figures is the only reality. We always have to take such care to find the right relationship between subjectivity and objectivity but we often find ourselves veering to one extreme or the other, unable to hold the two in creative tension. To counter this we have to recapture the ability to use our God-given imagination aright.

In history, we have repeated examples of the gift of imagination or intuition guiding people through such dilemmas and leading them into new eras. Studies of creative breakthrough in perception have shown us that in order for new understandings to be gained, it is sometimes necessary for seemingly unrelated experiences to be held together for a moment in the mind's eye. The falling of an apple on Newton's head and the lifting of the kettle lid as James Watt looked on, are tales that all schoolchildren are acquainted with. We remember too how Archimedes' bath strangely helped him make that imaginative leap into the world of physics and Gutenberg's reflections on the wine press helped him to take printing technology onto another plane. These moments of truth, when two seemingly unrelated things are brought together side by side and whole new perceptions pop into focus, are real creative breakthroughs.[6] The same seems to happen in all manner of creative discovery, be it in the world of physics, visual arts, poetry or chemistry and we too can participate in this dynamic in our theological explorations. Our critical imagination is fostered by placing alongside our common experiences of society, insights, pictures and stories, which come to us from various other sources and disciplines.

The most productive source that we found in our group often proved to be the Bible, since the stories told there have already proved their worth in this regard for those who have gone before us in Christian history. Our initial consideration of the imaginative stories told by Jesus, brought to our attention the fact that the very word 'parable', deriving as it does from the Greek for 'comparison', says in its own way much of what we were seeking after here. The parables of Jesus are fine examples of the dynamic of the imaginative and critical comparison of which we have been speaking, and so we decided that if our group were to have a name, then it should certainly have this word 'parable' included within it.

(iii) To do action theology

A third understanding which grew up amongst us is again certainly nothing new, but likewise difficult to accomplish and rarely adhered to, even by those who give so much lip-service to it. The old saying sums it up nicely: 'I hear and I forget, I see and I remember, I do and I understand.' Robert Holman tells the story[7] of a woman who was poverty stricken and atrociously housed. She, like so many, had become passive in her relationship with a Local Government Council who owned her accommodation and refused to maintain it as they should. She was then by chance invited to join a neighbourhood committee. It was new to her experience but soon she saw the committee standing up against the Council and she realised that, in comparison, her own personal response had been too subservient in the past. She accordingly demanded an interview with the Housing Manager and generally made herself a nuisance to him until her request was heard. Her toilet was quickly repaired! The learning process that this woman experienced was a complex of action and reflection. She *acted* in joining a committee. She *reflected* upon their style. She *reflected* upon her own. She *acted* upon her new perception and she thus confirmed what she had learnt from her membership of the committee. The action elicited new experience from which she no doubt learnt. We, like her, can only really learn by involving ourselves fully in the dynamic of subject and object, by *a unity of action and reflection*. Our group had to be constituted so that it would become not just a 'talk-shop' and not just an 'action group' but a careful amalgam of both aspects of learning. We therefore determined to call the group the 'Parables in Action' group.

(iv) To respect one another's experience

We had all had experiences of being in groups where our contribution had not been respected. Here it would be different. Each member knew that they had something to contribute from their life's experiences and would be given opportunity to share that in whatever way they found they could. There was plenty of straight talking and members were not pampered or patronised but a sensitivity to each person's worth was maintained which enabled each to make their point well. This called for a lot of careful listening and affirming but was kept in perspective by plenty of humour and relaxation together. The ethos became that of democratic dialogue and never was one member of our group allowed to elevate herself or himself above the others. We were all learners together, although some were called upon to fulfil particular functions in order that that could proceed well. Skills, weaknesses, strengths and failures, were all offered into the life of the group and used as the occasion demanded.

Such was the ethos and style of the group. The intention was that the dialogue style be fostered and the critical method be foremost in what we now called our Parables in Action group.[8] It seemed to us both a productive and a fair method of operation. But how did it work in practice?

C. Our first look at parables

At the first meeting, I set the ball rolling myself by asking, 'What does the Parable do? How does it work?'

To begin with, we listed all the biblical parables we could immediately recall. There were differences of opinion when someone asked whether the pastoral and rural pictures used in Jesus' parables made the stories irrelevant to our own industrial situation. With my own cockney upbringing, I recalled that I had not myself seen a lamb until I was turned twenty, so I for one had to recognise that the biblical context certainly differed drastically from our own. And yet we could all appreciate how significant or telling the stories were then, and how, despite the cultural gap between their original setting and ours, they remain stories which stir the imagination today. What seemed to make them so fascinating was that Jesus was able to take a situation and then give a twist to the story so that the hearers saw a familiar thing in a different light. That shift of understanding seemed to derive from the fact that Jesus was all the time using his parables to talk about the Kingdom of God. This observation was made by Fred who was the Anglican Churchwarden and who made tyres at the local Fort Dunlop factory. Jesus' stories derived from a depth of spiritual and theological vision which his everyday experience had made his own, and Fred was concerned that we would not understand Jesus' parables if we separated them off from the context of his life, work and other teaching.

In the Parables there were two elements in dynamic; firstly, there was Jesus' clear insight into the reality of the situation

around him, the history and make-up of the people, the
psychology and sociology of his place and time. Secondly, he
had a distinctive appreciation of the traditions and history of
his people as a religious community, his own sense of the
will and nearness of God, and his conviction of the present
and imminent reality of the Kingdom of Heaven. It was his
dynamic mix of these two elements which gave the parables
that fascinating twist in the tail and made them so effective
as tools in the cut and thrust of debate and conflict with the
authorities. They were tools to set the imagination to work
so that we might begin to see the 'alternative' within reality,
the alternative which can become the pivot for effective
change.[9]

The group was very practical by nature and believed
strongly that if we were to understand properly how parables
work then we would have to go through the process of parable
ourselves, rather than merely debate the model. For the
coming months, therefore, we set for ourselves this same
two-fold task; firstly, to look carefully again at our situation
in life, to consider our community, its history, its structure,
and people; and secondly, simultaneously and imaginatively
to reflect upon what God wanted us to be and do in that
situation. This we did, hoping that we would be able to bring
the two to bear one upon the other, just as Jesus himself
seemed to do so dynamically and critically in his parables.
We set about our new task with great enthusiasm.

D. Why our history is important

The Parables in Action group decided to look first at the
history of our place and its people before exploring its present
life and structures. It is not unusual for the Christian faith
to stress the importance of history in this way, for in the
making, development and interpretation of theologies there
is always an historical backbone on which other factors hang.
Much of the biblical record itself is a specialised historical
form, written from the perspective of those who are
convinced of God's liberating activity in history, although
this record is often overlaid with historical perspectives of

later biblical editors who appear to obscure the original
insight to suit their own theological purpose.[10] Again, we
are aware of the importance of the historical perspective
in the making of Christian doctrine. No-one will hope to
understand Christian dogma without a thorough background
in Church history, with all the political intrigue that went
with it. As the Parables in Action group began its grapplings
with our local history, we had to beware of straying too
far towards a subjectivism which might ignore both the felt
experiences of other groups and the realities of the political
and historical 'facts', as we sometimes call them. On the
other hand, no history is objective, for as soon as we look to
see what is or has happened, so we immediately interpret and
make it subjective by the very fact of our previous decision as
to where and how we look at it. We therefore determined to
see our history in terms of 'story', for story is the dynamic
interplay of the object and subject, of happening and
interpretation.

One aim of story is to begin to understand our own place
in history. The very important Old Testament phrase 'A
wandering Aramean was my father'[11] has converted an
historical *statement* about genealogy into a *story* about our
place in a 'history of salvation'. The poetic form of the
phrasing involves *me* at a personal level of response and,
especially if I am a Jewish reader, affirms my roots. As the
Hebrew Scriptures unfold, so the geographical place, the
Land, is stressed repeatedly until the Jewish reader knows
clearly where he or she belongs in the story. From the vantage
point of understanding our origins, our present situation and
its circumstances, and the forces of geography, sociology,
politics and spirituality on history, we can perceive more
clearly, and appreciate our role in the liberating line of
history. It is the 'story so far' which drives us to write the
next chapter for ourselves.

Once the news was out that the Parables in Action group
were to make a study of the history of our own community,
the interest in the work of the group blossomed. Newspaper
cuttings and snippets of information poured in. Maps, photo-
graphs and memoirs flooded round the various church groups
and meetings. The local Community Centre became engaged

and the story began to take shape. The city library saw many
a busy hour searching out old documents and books, and
tape recordings of ageing residents filled out many previously
unrecorded details. Many meetings of the Parables in Action
group took place, and as pieces began to slot into place in
the story, so interest increased, new members became
involved and all too often it was difficult to draw busy meetings to a close at a reasonable hour because of the interest
generated.

E. Our story: the historical survey

Our first problem stemmed from the fact that it was difficult
to give our story a name. Were we to call it a history of
Erdington, of Gravelly Hill, of Birches Green, or Erdington
Hall? Different structures and authorities used differing
names for our area. We seemed to be situated in a no-man's
land straddled between connecting police divisions, political
wards and postal areas. From the perspective of others we
were not understood to be a cohesive community in our own
right at all, just 'that area with lots of problems!' Erdington
was the name we fixed upon for ourselves as it meant most
to the majority of our members and our investigation of the
derivation of that name soon had us delving into our Saxon
roots. We found out that in 714 A.D., it had been called
Aedinton and the name seemed to refer to our area specifically. That old Saxon name described 'a hamlet in an
enclosed pasture'. It was nice to know that so early in
recorded history we were 'on the map'. As we searched back
through history, so more and more we felt that sense of
belonging and identity. We found, much to our astonishment,
that although today our area may be considered as the down-
town part of Erdington, it had been no mere after-thought,
but the original settlement area of the Norman period. We
even discovered a mention in the Domesday Book.[12]

The Parables in Action group used a loose-leaf file book
and kept adding historical information as we came across it,
until a full picture emerged from these earliest recorded
beginnings until the present day. We began by recording

anything that was known by the group of our early history. Whether it was true or not was not necessarily important at this juncture – we could always check that later, and in any case sometimes our stories proved more accurate than the learned history books which we found in the library. For example, on studying early maps, the facts could often be verified. We asked ourselves why we thought Erdington had become so important to Birmingham and we really could not fathom out why until we had pieced our whole story together. A large scale Government Ordnance Survey map of the area was obtained and by overlaying transparent acetate sheets it was possible to draw the details onto them from older maps to show the historical development and relative positions of the features at varying intervals from as early as 1576 to the present day. As later sheets were laid over preceding ones, so the group began to see how the area had been developed and could begin to guess at why things had happened as they had. Details were copied from early enclosure maps. From these we could see quite clearly the importance of the early bridging points across the River Tame at precisely the point where our more modern local bridge now stood. In those early times, the old bridge had allowed Birmingham access to the important Chester Road, a road which shows traces of Roman legionary use as the Empire's main route from London to the North – the famous Icknield Street. We enjoyed tracing the history of our area still further on and slowly began to realise that Erdington obviously had had no abundance of natural resources at any time but its importance had always lain in the simple fact of its accessibility and its location at this major route intersection at the two bridging points over the River Tame. We therefore focused in more carefully upon our importance as a communication centre. We traced the details of the building of the local canals and discovered how they had brought an abundance of light industry to our area. Likewise, the advent of the local railway had affected the area considerably as large houses of Victorian and Edwardian elegance clustered around the local Gravelly Hill station, where wealthy families came to live on the hill above the bustling industrial city. The history of the local tramways held a strange fascination for our group too and hours seemed to be lost in reminiscences of tram routes and numbers, and the journeys which had been taken years ago by some of our members to and from work each day. From the 1920s onward, the area saw extensive house-building programmes as artisans were drafted in to keep the wheels of the booming industry turning. One of our members, Ray, a jobbing builder, could work out for us which builders were responsible for which streets by referring to the makers' names on the porcelain in all the outdoor loos! He could also testify to the poor construction of many of the houses on these estates. We managed to trace the records of much of the construction of these sub-standard properties and found that local industrialists and builders had made a lively profit on these developments. The local Wheelwright Estate was built in this fashion and is now largely in the hands of the City Housing Department. The estate certainly has an extremely bad name with the authorities as a centre of violence and a haven for their so-called 'problem families', although those of us who lived there thought this picture to be not entirely fair. Industry had flourished in this period, the gigantic Fort Dunlop Tyre Factory had opened in 1916 and the vast Vickers Armstrong plant was later established nearby. Some of the group could remember much of this industry being turned over to armaments manufacture during the Second World War. Later still came British Leyland's vast car-body plant where some of our number now worked. The British Steel Corporation's tubes works likewise grew so vast as to become the biggest user of industrial gas in the whole of the West Midlands. We estimated that no less than one third of the geographical area of the St. Chad's parish is now taken up by this belt of industrial development.

We noted that over the years the descendants of the early wealthier inhabitants had moved north, leaving their grand houses to be redeveloped as hostels, guest-houses or flats. During the post-war boom, many immigrants arrived from the Caribbean, attracted by our government's and industry's promises of a new and exciting future in the 'Mother Country'. They were soon disillusioned, as we heard when the black members of our group shared their stories of the

high expectations and great disappointments of those early
years.[13] Many Irish and Eastern European families came
into the area too, and attended the nearby Roman Catholic
churches in Erdington itself. But the majority of the
community were originally drawn from the area of housing
further into the City Centre, particularly where areas of slum
property were demolished after the Second World War.

This constant process of change and movement has meant
that it would be difficult to conceive of an area more mixed
in style and demography. And this continuing development
more recently was evidenced in the building of the vast
motorway interchange, colloquially known as Spaghetti Junction, bringing with it the devastation of the west end of our
community, the demolition of important shopping facilities
and the introduction of more noise, lead pollution and road
danger.

The Parables in Action group brought all this historical
material together. Masses of pictures, maps, newspaper
cuttings as well as the written history were repeatedly
presented to others and to ourselves. We were aware of our
place as we had never been before. We were becoming aware
of the fact that decisions had been made and actions taken
which now profoundly affected our lives, yet rarely had those
decisions or actions been taken or initiated locally. The
importance of our locality to the industrial well-being of the
city and to the daily commuters, traders and travellers, could
not have been more clearly demonstrated. But there was a
tension between this importance and our actual lack of power
as a seemingly insignificant part of Erdington and of our city.
Because Jesus always noticed the unnoticed and celebrated
the non-celebrities, the feeling grew that we were living in a
place where we could expect what we called 'Kingdom reversals' to occur – where God could make the unexpected
happen.

F. Our community portrait

The Parables in Action group were asking questions of our
history; it was an exercise in raising our critical conscious-

ness. We had asked: 'What can be affirmed from our past? What from our past do we denounce? Which developments were good and which bad? Who made the decisions and who did they affect?' We wrote these questions in capital letters on paper that we stuck all around the walls of our meeting room. The story of our past was used as a springboard for our creative imagination.

But the past is not all we have from which to reflect forward, and it was clear that a study of the present realities would now need to be undertaken.[14] Already, our locality had been intensely surveyed by a number of outside bodies on various occasions, and students would often come and ask questions and write their reports about what they called this 'deprived area'. Rarely, if ever, had any stayed for longer than it had taken to write their reports and local residents had never heard about any of their findings. We felt like animals in a zoo! Our feelings of indignation as a group served to make us wary of treating our community similarly, as if our community were a decaying body ready for post-mortem.

We were also aware that the regular surveying of the community and the specifying of its ongoing problems could lead to despair if the latest survey did not evidence any improvement since the last one. This task had therefore to be undertaken with great sensitivity.

Marjorie, one of our group, set about collating all the reports we could lay our hands on and added in the details from the masses of demographic material with which the planning department of the City of Birmingham were pleased to supply to us.[15] With that work in hand, the group then felt able to go about looking at our area in our own more subjective way. Thirteen members of our now enlarged group volunteered to look specifically at areas immediately around their own homes and to report back their findings. In this way, a good cross-section of the community would be covered and we would be able to report our own feelings before we were bombarded with the wealth of the objective data which Marjorie was still amassing.

We needed some sort of check-list to get us started. Rather than use a set of questions produced by outside agencies, we felt it to be quite important that we asked our own questions in our own way. We hoped thereby that 'suburban' assumptions would be less likely to colour our judgements about our own area, for we had already been offended by some of the questions which had appeared in surveys that had been visited upon our area in the past. Our discussion therefore ranged through the sorts of questions which we felt were important, and I was asked from that guide to draw up a check-list we could all use. This was soon duplicated and distributed and individuals drew in friends and neighbours and relatives to help make some assessment of their immediate patch. The first questions in the list of seventeen were as follows:-

1. Walk casually in your patch and get the feel of it afresh. How does it strike you today? Warm and welcoming, threatening, cared for? Is there pride in the community, or is it run down? On the up or on the down?

2. Now look closely at the street. Are there shops, houses, factories, offices, etc.? What functions do the buildings serve? Are they used, derelict or empty?

3. Are they expensive to occupy? Guess how much a family would have to have coming in, to live here without financial struggle.

4. What about the people? Young children, elderly, black, white, single, married?

5. Do any particular people stand out? Who do people go to in an emergency? Any important people here? What makes them important?

6. Are there neighbourhood tensions?

And so this list of questions went on until most subjects were touched upon. The questions were 'ways in' to our own thinking about our own community, for we already had masses of objective statistics coming in from our other enquiries. The walls of our meeting room were soon covered with charts of our findings. Roads were compared, tensions discussed, trends noticed. Strengths and positive features were celebrated and fears and depressions shared.

On our large community map we marked all the institutions and amenities, and group members opted personally to investigate each one whenever we found that we were not already well informed. Extra information came in from various sources. Colin, by virtue of his many years of commitment to the youngsters of our Boys' Brigade and Youth Clubs, had built up a good deal of wisdom about our community and he offered to ask local youngsters their opinions about our area. Jack, a milkman, a trades unionist and deeply committed Methodist, fascinated us with unbelievable information about the natural wildlife of the area, including magpies, foxes and moles! Madeleine, a secretary with great knowledge of the church and the community, brought in details of the local Community Centre where she was an active member and Ron, a local union official, presented us with a brilliant photographic portrait of the community, 'warts and all'. After four long months of intensive investigation, our portrait of the community, its people and structures, was complete.

We were very much aware that our critical and questioning approach had been paying dividends, for we were beginning to see that by virtue of asking new questions of the community we thought we had known so well, we were uncovering facts to which we had perhaps turned a blind eye in the past.

We had looked afresh at the population figures, the ethnic mix, the overcrowded accommodation in many areas of the parish and the anxiety the residents felt about the deterioration of the fabric and the delinquency and violence on the streets. We had to accept the findings of the government reports that twenty percent of households were without, or having to share, an inside WC and that tenants faced many other basic problems and challenges, not least in relation to the authorities. We were not at all happy with the constant reference to the low moral and intellectual standards of our people – and so often the derogatory phrase 'problem families' was scattered through these reports. We knew our area had long been designated as an Educational Priority Area but even we were amazed to see how high the unemployment rate had climbed, that the poverty was such that far more than half of our schoolchildren were allowed to receive their school meals free of charge, and that twenty-six percent of our population reported that the only social life they could manage was television viewing. The air pollution figures around the busy Spaghetti Junction gave us great cause for concern, as did the realisation that access to any open space or grassed areas was very severely limited for people in our area. We seemed to be hemmed in by very fast and dangerous commuter roads, a reminder of our long history as a communication routeway.

Perhaps never before had we appreciated as we did now the tremendous pressures upon the people of our parish and yet many times we still said to one another in the group – 'Yes, but it's still home to us, isn't it; it's got lots of faults but it's good to be living in such a lively and bustling little community.'

What hit us most was the simple fact that most of us church people had not really appreciated the difficulties which beset so many of our parishioners. Although many of the group had lived here nearly all their lives, there was so much we had not been aware of before. We had even found out that in one street things were so bad that as many as forty-five percent of those living there had applied to the Council to get out of the area 'as soon as possible'. After so much careful historical analysis and after having drawn up our in-depth profile of the community, we perceived that whilst much was to be affirmed in our parish, there were still four or five main issues which concerned us greatly and about which we felt something needed to be done.

Firstly, and most importantly, we, the people of the church, felt we had allowed our church to become distant from the experience and needs of the people of our community. Secondly, there was a clear impression coming through from our findings that most of the policy decisions made about our community and its people were always made by those outside the community, with little or no consultation with the residents whose lives those decisions affected. Thirdly, the helping organisations, both statutory and voluntary, were straining and struggling to maintain themselves and were achieving very little forward movement for the improvement of the community and its people. Fourthly, the information and skills needed to operate the structures and gain the much-needed help were rarely at the disposal of those most in need. Many went without simply because they were unaware help was available, or else were not sure how to get it. And finally, we felt that the perceptions which residents had of the causes of their difficulties or the difficulties of their neighbours were limited to rather self-denigrating ideas they has been fed by popular myth and biased media. Rarely had causes been properly thought through.

There only remained now the task of making a proper assessment of ourselves in order to make our survey of our situation complete. We set about this with the same commitment to detail and integrity that had been evident in our other research. We wrote up a history of our three churches and told the story of our more recent denominational unity. We looked at our resources, our membership, at the long list of clubs and activities which we sponsored. We considered the structure of our church decision-making arrangements. We had for some time determined to include the whole congregation as much as possible in decision-making by means of a number of lay-chaired committees which were responsible for all aspects of the life of the church and we were pleased to see, on reflection, how well this democratisation had worked out. While we were making a careful assessment of the whole ministry of St. Chad's, this seemed to be a good opportunity to ask the group to monitor and assess my own part in that ministry as vicar of the parish. This they did very systematically and thoroughly. The group turned out to be very supportive despite their sharp honesty and whilst they helped me to understand my gifts and weaknesses, they in turn heard from me how I perceived the priestly role and how I attempted to fulfil it within the overall ministry at St. Chad's.

The outcome of this self-assessment of our church and its ministry left us feeling generally positive about our internal church structures, the spiritual commitment of our members, and our ecumenical unity. All this was despite the fact that we were indeed very few in number and in many ways only a very insignificant back-street church. There was certainly evidence of strong individual relationships between our church members and the community in which we were set, and there was no doubt that St. Chad's had been well blessed in so many ways. But we felt that the time had now come for our united congregation to relate more closely *as a body* to the evident needs of the area.

We had had a little success on this front before. We had in the past campaigned and won the battle against the City Planning Department for certain roads, which had been made one-way only, to be reopened to the community. We had run a number of schemes by which local residents were made aware of our commitment to the Gospel of Christ and encouraged to join our worship. We had taken a leading part in pushing for the provision of a Community Centre in the locality separate from the church and this had enabled the church to remain in the servant role rather than for it to appear itself to be the centre of the community. It seemed to us, in our secular urban setting, that to purport to be the centre of the community would have contradicted the New Testament mandate to be the servant.

But, having done that, how were we now going to fulfil this call to the Christian servant role? We all sensed that there was the necessity for something fundamentally new. We had learnt new things about our situation, about our distance from the chronic needs of our neighbours, and about our own longing to find ways of relating to our fellow men and women which respected their needs but did not deny that they had things to teach us about the Gospel too.

Having carefully analysed the situation around us, we now had to try to discern God's will for us within it. This called for careful theological reflection.

3: Making Some Sense Of Our Situation

A. God's unexpected

You will recall that this whole process of action and reflection had started from the group's fascination to see how parables operate in the Bible. Everybody knows that Jesus' parables, when taken at even the simplest level, are remarkably compelling stories. I had to tell the group that even now I can remember from my earliest childhood seeing a student-teacher acting out in front of our enormous class the story of the Unjust Steward. I can picture vividly in my mind how that young teacher with a paper quill wrote down the debts of those who owed his master money, and my great surprise to hear that Jesus commended this rogue after all because, as the teacher explained, at least he had done something about the crisis he was in and didn't just mope about it. What a gripping tale it had been!

Sometimes, the Parables in Action group diplomatically ignored my hare-brained suggestions, but this time there was enough support to try a little drama. We took a character each and acted our way through a few parables – after all, there was no-one watching, except ourselves. We tried some parables that we knew well, The Prayers of the Pharisee and the Tax-Collector, The Labourers in the Vineyard and The Wise and Foolish Virgins. The strange thing that we had not bargained for was that, after each parable had been acted out and some of the emotions and thoughts of the characters had been experienced 'from the inside' so to speak, then at least one of the character players felt upset in each case. In abstract, we all knew the stories well, but acting them out in this concrete fashion brought home to us as never before that in each parable there is a 'twist in the tail' and often a character who began in the story with great expectations ended up disappointed. Even those who had not had a part to play began to look out for this unexpected twist in the story. We began to go through in our minds as many parable stories as we could, to see if they always had an unexpected outcome. We found that although in each case the twist was of a slightly different nature, there nevertheless always was one. In the parable of the Prodigal Son, there was no doubt in our minds that the love and acceptance shown by the father towards the squandering and self-seeking prodigal was most extraordinary. The story of the Sower told us that some seed yielded grain far in excess of anything ever dreamt of in those days, despite the haphazard method of sowing which the story describes. The villainous steward who defrauds his employer[1] turns out to be the hero! The servant who safeguards his master's talent and returns it to him safely[2] ends up being called a good-for-nothing!

'But all this is just typical of Jesus', said Marjorie, 'whatever he teaches and whatever he does, it's always the opposite of what you expect! I mean, you don't really expect him to be crucified, or even born in a stable if he's the Messiah, do you?'

It was then I remembered once seeing my close friend and mentor, the Reverend Dr John Vincent,[3] draw a diagram in which as each element in Jesus' life was charted, so alongside was stated how different His story was from that which we would have expected. We decided to do some such thing for ourselves. We called it 'Looking for God's Unexpected'. We carefully listed some of the basic elements in the Gospel story, such as Jesus' birth, his disciple group, his symbolic actions, his death, his resurrection, and so on. Under each of these headings we considered whether or not we could discern an unexpected or unusual quality in the event or happening and how that might resonate with our own experience.

Repeatedly we were taken aback by the same unexpected 'twist' which we had discerned in the parable stories of Jesus. All the normal ideas of status and pedigree were exploded by the 'unexpected' circumstances of Jesus' birth. Next, we were newly surprised to see how Jesus had called working class fishermen, women of questionable profession and, judging by their names, those who had belonged to terrorist organisations, into his discipleship group.[(4)] It seemed to us then that working class people really did have some special place in Jesus' heart and mind even if the Church of England today was predominantly middle and upper class. In the healing stories of Jesus, we saw him going out of his way to empower those who normally would have been little noticed – and what a surprise it was to see Jesus actually bringing health even on the days when the Sabbath Law forbad it! Next, all our accepted notions of leadership were made to stand on their head by many of the symbolic activities in which we saw Jesus engaging. He washed his disciples' feet, he rode on a donkey, he submitted to baptism – time and again the leader was seen as servant. With the crucifixion and the resurrection stories before us, we could only wonder at the self-giving of the man, and then, the totally unexpected affirmation in the resurrection that with God everything is possible.

Because it was Ascension week, we finished our chart off with some reflection on the unexpected that this implied.

'I suppose', said Sue, 'that it's odd that Jesus doesn't stay forever. He leaves us again at the Ascension. He doesn't come back and 'take over'. He gives us responsibility and gives us a chance too, while at the same time giving his spirit to help us.'

The chart was complete. At every turn of Jesus' life, there was the underlying factor that with the Kingdom of God operating you have to expect God's Unexpected to turn all our human assumptions on their head. It was inevitable then that in the parable stories the twist in the tail is always unexpected, because Jesus makes the story conform to the Kingdom of God vision of how things must be.

B. Checking our stories against New Testament stories

The parables, we had noted, were stories which compared normal human expectations with the Kingdom's expectations – hence the twist in the tail of each of them. At the next of our meetings we therefore tried our hand at bringing well-known gospel stories alongside our own experience, to see similarities or dissimilarities which might spark our imagination and reproduce the twist. At random, we took stories we knew well. Some passages, such as the story of the Widow's Mite[5] and Jesus' sayings about children[6] prompted rather simplistic observations and we realised that great care would have to be taken in using biblical material in this way, because lifting stories out of context like this might completely muddle their meaning. Nevertheless, we did find that many passages would really spark our imagination, as for example when we looked at the very well-known parable of the Good Samaritan.[7] As it was acted and read out, a number of parallels with our own situation became startlingly clear.

Firstly, there was a clear parallel between the seriousness of the situation in the story and in our community. The man who had 'fallen among thieves' was almost symbolic to our mind of those in our community. The very community itself seemed to have been the victim of thieves throughout its long history.

Next, we observed that the Priest and the Levite in the story were not allowed to help even if they had really wanted to, because the rules and taboos which governed their society forbade it. Those who were about to participate in the Jerusalem Temple worship, as they were, were in no way allowed to come into contact with this half dead man since that would have contaminated them, leaving them ritually impure. The Law expected that they should keep as far distant as 'the other side of the road' would allow. Our community profile told us that in our society too there were rules and regulations like this which overburdened and constrained even those whose very task supposedly was to be of assistance to those in need. We had found many times that officialdom and red-tape bound up the helping agencies and those in need were passed on from department to department, referred to as 'clients' and 'cases', until they felt abused and inclined to give up. Sometimes, this would lead to a fearful sense of isolation, and although we celebrated the fact that there were in our locality lots of good informal networks and grapevines, the weakest of our people had become so isolated that they were not even in touch with these supports of care and neighbourliness. Sometimes, it seemed that in our society we had all become so privatised that we did not even want to know our neighbours any more, or perhaps our experiences had made us feel that the world was no longer trustworthy and this had led to even more fear, isolation and defensive red-tape. It was such isolation, we perceived, which compounded poverty and oppression.

'But the very acceptable thing about the Good Samaritan', continued Colin, whose insurance office job had taught him all about red-tape and security, 'is that he sees a clear need and just gets on and helps in a very concrete fashion. Even though a Samaritan isn't supposed to touch a Jew, he sees a man in need so he ignores the awful apartheid law and gets on with it.'

It seemed to our group that all our lives long we had heard that areas like ours had no indigenous leadership or skills – we had heard it so often that we were even inclined to believe it ourselves, despite the fact that there was plenty of evidence to the contrary. We could see a clear need in our community and could see that the official structures of our society were too overburdened to be of much help. We knew we should do something but felt inadequate, unskilled and unprofessional.

'But surely, if even the unlikely Samaritan could manage to do something . . . then why not us?' asked Louise hesitantly.

Although Jesus' hearers would not have expected it, the 'unworthy' Samaritan did have resources as well as the will to offer them and we were reminded by our earlier community survey that we too had resources which could serve in a very down-to-earth way. We already had a thriving community grape-vine, lots of contacts and a church and hall to offer. What we were still not sure of, was how to offer them although we were aware that many of our parishioners were not getting their rights because the necessary information and service was usually at a distance – geographically, culturally and financially – from where it was most needed.

'Well, we've said that one of the biggest problems here is that people don't, for all sorts of reasons, know how to get in contact with the help they need', thought Madeleine aloud, 'so surely we could act as some sort of bridge or a link. Just like the Samaritan, we are actually where the parishioners are, we're right on the spot. Even if we could only act as an information centre for people, that would be something.'

We were led by John to notice that the Samaritan scored in another way too. Unlike our State Welfare, the help he offered in no way left the sufferer in a dependent corner. The Welfare State machine was apt to trap the individual or family in a disabled situation of poverty and dependence which in the long run really was far from helpful and empowering. Whatever we did, we would have to be careful to follow the Samaritan's example and help without disabling. An information centre, it seemed, might give resources and contacts to people so that they could then take charge of their own lives in a more liberating way.

Jim, another member of the group, was concerned that whatever we did would have to take proper notice of how Jesus had introduced this parable in order to bring a lofty theological discussion down to earth, for as St. Luke records it,[8] there are in this account two people in need, not one. There is of course the man who fell among thieves in the parable, but there is also the lawyer who had originally asked Jesus the question which had prompted the telling of the story: 'Master, what must I do to inherit eternal life?' Jesus replies, in effect, that since the questioner is a theologian and lawyer then he should be able to work this out for himself. The lawyer replies by reciting the two basic elements of the Old Testament Code, 'Love the Lord your God . . . and your neighbour as yourself.[9] 'There you are', says Jesus, 'you knew all the time; go and do it and all will be well.' But the lawyer is more keen to be seen to be a professional theologian than actually to put the Law into practise and so he makes the whole thing into a debate by asking the further question about who the neighbour is and how far the law of neighbourliness should extend. As with all theologians of the wrong sort, the lawyer wants to keep everything at the level of abstraction and is reluctant to acknowledge that the answers to his questions are better worked out in practical service. The Parables group was only too aware how easy it would be to become patronising and theoretical in this way and constantly stressed the difference in their experience between those who did good *to* others and those who worked *with* others to see good prevail.

Although we had made very broad and liberal use of the parable of the Good Samaritan, it seemed that our discussion had eventually focused in upon the central meaning of the whole story and we had become critically aware that it was the reality and the quality of our love and servanthood which the parable was holding up for inspection. It questioned whether we were really alongside those in our community who were most hurt by society's ills and it challenged us further to find ways of being of service which were neither patronising, exclusive nor self-centred.

C. Getting our objectives clear

Although we had gained so much from the story of the Good Samaritan, we were aware, of course, that imaginative insights would be gained from many other biblical and secular sources too and so we kept our horizons wide. We considered many different parable stories as they seemed to parallel the issues we had discovered during the analysis of our community. Each and every time, we seemed to be led to think that an information and advice centre would be the obvious project in which to engage. Although its setting up seemed quite a daunting prospect for us, it did have the advantage of probably being manageable, given the very limited resources that our little church had at its disposal.

'What I like most about this idea,' said Sue 'is that I can see this information centre or advice bureau giving us a chance to get at that fifth issue which our community faces. There is so much suffering and no one understands the basic causes for it. The people who are suffering don't understand, we as a group don't understand, and I certainly don't understand! *Why* there is so much suffering in our community is the real theological question!'

The advice bureau idea certainly did seem to give us an opportunity of engaging with the suffering in our community, of being alongside people in their experience of it and perhaps understanding more of its causes. But if we were going to learn through the experience in this way, it was going to be important that we not only spent time on developing the information centre itself but that we also allowed proper time for this theological reflection to take place simultaneously. In this way, we would at each stage of our development be thinking carefully about what we had done in the project and informing our next action by our careful reflection on our experience so far. It would be a circle of action and reflection – what the scholars sometimes called 'dialectical education'.[10] It also occurred to us that if the project did offer us opportunity to get alongside and listen carefully to suffering people, and if our constant reflection helped us and them to understand some of the underlying causes of that suffering, then it would be possible for us together to initiate political action for the betterment of the locality. To some small extent this might enable the local people to take more initiative in the decision-making process of the community. If that happened, it would be doing something directly to alleviate one of the issues that had cried out to us during our historical analysis of the area: that decisions about the community had rarely, if ever, been made by the people those decisions were to affect.

In some senses, we realised that we could not claim really to have begun to 'do theology' until we had embodied what we had so far learnt and got some feedback from that. It was undoubtedly superficial learning up to now but here was an opportunity to learn much more from real experience. An advice centre run from St. Chad's in, for and by the community, as a self-consciously Christian parabolic action, offering information, advice and solidarity, would in turn teach us a great deal and this learning could be fed through to the church at large. There was a real chance therefore that this project could turn out to be the sort of consciousness-changing experience which we spoke of in the very first chapter of this book. Goals were set, objectives and strategies specified, and methods of evaluation worked out. After much discussion and fine tuning, we eventually arrived at a series of goals which we had very carefully worded, each goal with a fully stated rationale and a series of objectives for action which derived from it. When we felt we had our goals word perfect, we wrote them up on the walls of our discussion room.

This is what the goals themselves eventually looked like:

First goal

To begin the engagement of our church group in the process of liberation with those in our community who are oppressed by our society's structures.

The establishment of a group, acting in concert with other concerned people, to operate a Community Advice Centre, open to all, which is effectively engaged where people are hurt.

Second goal

To embody the concern and present understanding of the nature of oppression which we, a theologically reflective group, have thus far developed.

This Community Advice Centre is created as a sacramental or parabolic action as self-consciously as possible.

Third goal

To enable all those participating in the project in any way, who wish to be engaged in further reflection, to grow in their theological understanding.

Allowing this reflective Parables in Action group both to share in the experience of those being most hurt and actively to reflect upon this new incarnation of ourselves.

Fourth goal

To begin the process of making the wider congregation and the wider Community Advice Centre participants aware of this new learning.

The Parables in Action group would be sharing this new learning with the wider congregation and the Community Advice Centre team.

The formation of these four goals was a lengthy process but we were keen to be precise about our aims so that when we were later engaged in the complex project we would not lose sight of the wood for the trees. We were very encouraged too when Marjorie reinforced our thinking by bringing to our attention the findings of one of those earlier government surveys of our area where it stated that no less than 87.6 per cent of local residents themselves had asked for the provision of just such a local information and advice service. There was much interest from all quarters in the project and the Parochial Church Council too were very affirmative of the scheme. What they liked about it was that it all related so clearly to the ongoing life of the whole church. It was not exclusive in any sense, membership of the group being drawn from all quarters within St. Chad's and so flexible that it was easy for folk to come along to a meeting or two whenever they could manage. There was a gratifying feeling that the project belonged to the whole church and was not just a group or club loosely sponsored by the church as so many such ventures easily can be. It was felt by all to be integrally related to the overall thrust of the church's education programme and its own ministry in the community.

The whole venture seemed very grand for such an unsophisticated group, but we were very pleased with our efforts over so many months. As we sat in the vicarage one evening looking at the four goals for the group, we began to appreciate what a daunting task we had set for ourselves and we soon found ourselves praying together again.

D. Getting organised

We were all alike new to advice centre work and it was only after many months of further rigorous planning and research that we became more fully aware of the dangers and pitfalls of the task we were undertaking. Our discussions with the Citizens Advice Bureau[11] instilled into us the importance of the accuracy of information to be shared, of the co-operative nature of advising and the importance of the continuing training of the volunteers. On the other hand, we were aware that the local community-based nature of our project was inevitably going to make our Centre somewhat different from theirs in character, for our volunteer advisers were all to be local and mainly working class people.

Our conversations with Margaret Selby, a church worker who had been the organiser of the Lane Neighbourhood Centre in an old inner city area of Birmingham, reminded us that any advice agency had to earn its right to respect and for us there would be the added problem that people coming to the church for advice could well see the project as just a catch, a gimmick to attract people to worship. We considered this difficulty repeatedly in our early months of operation. Our discussions with Margaret also centred around our concern to find the right name for the project. The word 'Advice' sounded rather patronising and that certainly was not our intention, but as we asked around, the name 'Advice Centre' seemed to be the one to which our local people most readily responded, despite its obvious limitations. We wanted people to appreciate the local community nature of the project too, and so we finally settled for the title 'Community Advice Centre'.

It was clear to us that the centres which worked well had established a good co-operative working team but each had a supervisor, who co-ordinated the work. The group decided to ask the obvious person to take on this role. Madeleine had experience in secretarial work and administration and had been central to the Parables in Action group from the outset. She had lived in our locality for many years and had recently retired. She had developed a real feel for the locality and had a commitment that knew no bounds. After much heart-searching, she decided to give it a try. An assistant organiser was appointed too. Alan, a young family man who had a head for figures and a kindly, sensitive manner, agreed to act as deputy and as treasurer for the project. The church congregation heard about the project by word of mouth, by sermons on the subject and by a magazine article written by Alan which appeared in *Chad*, the parish monthly. It began as follows:-

'When you look at our community you may be struck by the need for a place where anybody can go along and be sure to be seen by someone who makes time to listen carefully to their problem and helps the person find out what they need to know. It may be a family matter, or difficulty with filling in forms, finding out about supplementary benefits, rent or rate rebates, legal advice, consumer advice, how to insulate their house – and all the many questions or problems that anyone might be faced with.

It's not always that easy to go into town for advice or to pluck up enough courage to go to a city centre advice bureau – so why not have one here . . . ?'

We were amazed at the ready response elicited by Alan's article. The idea was warmly welcomed from within the church and without, and many willing volunteers came forward from all quarters.

From this group, a working party was elected and given the job of moving the project along from the 'aims and objectives' stage to look at 'ways and means'. Was the project feasible in terms of our buildings? Would the funding be sufficient? Were the budgets credible? Were time-schedules and management structures sensitively drawn up in relation to the many personal and political hurdles that stood between us and our objective? The Chairperson of this working party was chosen from the congregation on the basis of his experience as a local Trades Union official, for he understood the importance of clear and flexible structures for management and the needs and skills of the volunteers. Ron was a fine figure-head for the project and presented himself confidently when personal negotiations with politicians, civil servants and funding agencies were entered into on behalf of the Advice Centre. His manner made it clear to those meeting him that the project, whilst certainly a grass-roots working-class project, had all the efficiency and direction of any professional group.

It was also tremendously exciting to see people who had not before been in positions of leadership and decision-making finding out that all they needed was determination and a little experience. My task was largely to encourage, to ask the awkward questions, to maintain unity and repeatedly to ask the group to check that what was happening was occurring through the will of the Spirit of God at work amongst us.

Maintaining unity was certainly not to be done through

evasion of any tensions and within the group we encouraged straight speaking. However, a growing spiritual maturity was very evident when we shared the eucharist or even a common meal together, and enabled the group to hold together through thick and thin. The project was proving to me that every community has its potential indigenous leadership but that potential has to be bravely encouraged, trained and empowered.

Ron ably steered the working party on its way and at a meeting of the Joint Church Council, the proposals presented by that working party were accepted without reservation and the appropriate local personnel were elected to become the Management Committee of the new Community Advice Centre. The project was at last formally constituted!

E. Personnel and training

Our study of the parable of the Good Samaritan and the evidence of our community portrait helped us to determine that the project was to be staffed and managed only by local volunteers rather than by the helping professionals who, like the Priest and Levite, might be limited by their red tape and class expectations.[12] We had also decided that we would try never to refer to people as 'clients' or 'cases', as the more bureaucratic organisations were inclined to, but would refer to our visitors in more personable terms.

Our intention was that our team of volunteer receptionists would welcome visitors and keep the tea-pot pouring, and this would make the Centre very relaxed and give a homely feel to the operation. Advisers would discuss the issues with the visitors and refer to the Information Pack to be kept in the Centre office. This Pack would hold information on the widest variety of subjects possible. From it the adviser and visitor would be able to draw the information they required in order to work out together the available strategies for action in the face of the issue raised. The likely consequences of each strategy would be discussed and hopefully the visitors given the wherewithal to make the best decision for themselves. We soon realised therefore that we would need a clerical team to update and augment the Information Pack which was to include a large filing system, many reference books and catalogues, forms and explanatory notes, card indexes of important telephone numbers and useful contacts.

It was necessary to set up training classes for all our volunteers and with this we were greatly assisted by the Citizens Advice Bureau, and by Frank, a local hospital chaplain. As well as learning interviewing skills and remembering basic rules such as confidentiality, it was also necessary to attend classes on welfare benefits, the Health Service, local authority structures and to learn a little about the British legal system. We had to become conversant with the files of information which we bought for the office and a whole network of odd-job personnel, van drivers, gardeners, old clothes and furniture resources. We knew too that many of our visitors would bring experience and skills which we did not have and they themselves would act as a great resource. The series of training classes once started could never cease, of course, since all the time new rules and regulations had to be learnt and understood, so the whole team of workers contracted to meet every fortnight from then on for continuing training. This early team of volunteers showed great commitment and courage! Some were even so committed to the project that they paid for their transport and training from their meagre personal savings.

F. The management function

Meanwhile, the Management Committee was progressing famously. As they gained confidence, so they proved that the whole project could be operated and managed by local people without having policy decisions made always by those outside the community. They saw to it that the office was properly equipped with the essential desks, typewriters, telephone and copying machines. The way in which they went about their business was so inspiring that other agencies were keen to help wherever they could; the local Labour Party, for example, helped to buy bright carpet tiles for the reception area where tea and coffee were to be served. The committee also negotiated a comprehensive insurance policy to cover all the workers and advisers, and they bought in the nationally produced Information Pack, together with an updating service. They negotiated with the Law Society for a special waiver of its rules so that willing solicitors could be available to offer their services free of charge to needy visitors. They designed, printed and distributed very attractive advertising material, so that the Community were kept informed of progress.

Preliminary discussions about management structures had been prolonged for we had learnt that other centres had been hampered by bad management or had even been taken over by over-efficient professionals. We had therefore determined that the power should always remain in the hands of the local people and the constitution had been written accordingly. Once the committee felt strong enough, representatives were invited from the local school, the Social Services Department, the Community Centre and the local Council. When any professionals were brought in, it was only to offer advice and counsel, but the power to make final policy decisions remained always with the community representatives.

It was clear from the outset that fund-raising was bound to prove difficult not only because of the general economic and industrial blight currently affecting British inner cities, but also because of government reluctance to fund advice centres which inevitably focussed upon the problems being faced by many people living in the urban areas. Some programmes had published research findings which had proved too radical for their government sponsors and had been drastically curtailed.[13]

How relieved we were then to receive a loan or grant for £250 from the Church of England Diocese of Birmingham through its Department of Social Responsibility. Our own St. Chad's Church Council offered another £100 loan and our Working Party were quick to hold a Jumble Sale which brought our total, along with other small donations from project members, to around £500. Alan, our treasurer, began to draw up realistic budgets for the first three years of operation based on the best advice we could find.

It was then possible to make formal application to a number

of charities and we prepared an information pack to describe our hopes and fears to these agencies. Early disappointing replies were indicative of the economic climate and it was a worrying time for such a poor community. At last, help came from two charitable trusts which allowed us to pay off loans and expand our training and advertising programmes. When, a little later, our application for Birmingham Inner City Partnership money proved successful, this gave us the confidence to feel that the project was now properly secure and under way.

What a lot we had learnt. It felt as if we had been paralysed for years and now we had been touched and inspired by Jesus' Kingdom alternatives and had been empowered to stand up and walk for ourselves. We were experiencing God's Unexpected.

4: Discovering How Parables Operate

We had to agree that throughout the long process of preparation and organisation of the Community Advice Centre, it had been right to keep reflecting theologically upon our aims and strategies. This reflection had been taking place informally at many levels and in many places but more specifically, it was the task which we had set for our Parables in Action group.

Having briefly described the way in which the Community Advice Centre was being organised, we now need to sketch out some of the fascinating discoveries which the Parables in Action group were making during this process.

Emily, who was one of the group, had spotted a television programme quite early on in the process of our discussions, which had been considering how in the world of scientific discovery, leaps can be made when a scientist comes up not with new information but with a new way of looking at the old information. Something pushed Emily to wonder whether this was similar in some senses to what we had been saying Jesus was doing with his parables. Were they not asking us to look to familiar situations but from a very new perspective? The group asked me to find out more about what these scientific parables might be so that we could compare them with biblical ones.

What I came up with was quite interesting and to the next meeting I was able to bring along a book by Thomas Kuhn, who had written not about parables, but paradigms.[1] According to Kuhn, a paradigm is a new and unprecedented mode of scientific observation, a new mind-set, which once discovered by a group of scientists allows them to go back to all the original observable data and learn totally new things from them. It's like finding a new key which allows hitherto unknown things to be discovered. A paradigm is not necessarily new information, but it is an excitingly refreshing way of piecing known information together. As we use this new pattern of understanding, so old data become fresh and then brand new data are newly discovered. Just as a biblical parable makes us look upon the world from a totally new and Godward perspective, seeing the old world afresh and discovering totally new things too, so the scientific paradigm brings a new perspective on scientific issues. It seemed to me that it was the *pattern of activity* within the paradigm which made one look for similar patterns of activity elsewhere. And biblical parables worked in a very similar way by making us look for newly discernable patterns of activity.

I explained to the group what I understood from all this. We first of all needed to appreciate that the parables of Jesus are introduced in the gospels in two different ways. Firstly there is the straightforward story format where there's plenty of movement and action as the story unfolds. But then there are those parabolic images such as the picture of the grain of mustard seed, which is not really a story form but a description. The key the scholars give us to understand this form is the fact that in the Greek, the language in which the Gospel stories come down to us in written form, such descriptive parables are introduced by a word in the dative case which probably translates an Aramaic phrase (Jesus' spoken language) which points the hearer to look at the active and moving aspects of the description. This is why Joachim Jeremias, one of the greatest parable scholars can say:

'In Matt 13:31 we should not . . . translate the introductory formula by "The Kingdom of God is like a grain of mustard seed" but "It is the case with the Kingdom of God as with a grain of mustard seed" i.e., the Kingdom of God is not compared to a grain of mustard seed but to the tall shrub in whose boughs the birds make their nests.'[2]

In the descriptive parables, just as in those which follow the story format, Jesus is offering us a *pattern of activity* as a paradigm for what we must expect to see when we see signs of God's Kingdom in his world. It seems to be the activity or dynamic in the parables which is compared so that the parables give us ways into seeing what is now likely to be happening in view of the new revolutionary Kingdom of God situation. So Emily had been right in thinking that scientific paradigms operate similarly to biblical parables, for both produce a radical shift in perspective. Just as the new scientific paradigm is presented as a typical example of how we may now expect things to operate, so the New Testament parable shows how, given the advent of the Kingdom, God's Unexpected must constantly be affirmed in order that the signs and activities of the Kingdom may be more clearly perceived and appreciated.

Having thought carefully through the similarities between the biblical parables and those in the scientific area, we turned our attention to the similarities between Jesus' parables and others which we could find in the Bible. In the Old Testament, all sorts of stories, proverbs and parables went under the Hebrew name *Māshāl* and it was this rather general word which in the New Testament was translated as 'parable'. So there were many stories and sayings of varying style and length in the Old Testament which we compared with the parables of Jesus. For example, we studied the story told by the Old Testament prophet Nathan to King David.[3] The story seemed to be a quite harmless tale about a man who had one single ewe lamb and about a rich man who stole the little lamb away. But once the story had the King's attention, he was then brought to realise that it was in fact an attack on his own behaviour – he was the rich man in the story!

'That certainly has the same feeling about it as Jesus' parables. His stories seem comfortable at first,' observed Joan, 'and then you realise they're making you rethink things about yourself.'

We read through many of the Old Testament parabolic sayings and acted out the stories to find that many of the themes which they stressed were reworked in the parables of Jesus. We also began to realise though, that Jesus was laying especial emphasis in his stories upon the immanence of God's Kingdom. The Kingdom challenged by its moral imperative and by its sheer urgency; but as Beryl pointed out, the parables of Jesus were doing a lot more than just telling us to behave ourselves. To take the parables as just moral fables would have been to follow in the footsteps of the great scholar of the last century, Adolf Jülicher.[4] He had quite rightly emphasised that the parables should not be split up into many pieces and allegorised point by point, for each parable, he believed, had one major point to make, not many. However, having discovered that, Jülicher then went on to make the mistake of claiming that the one central point was always a moral principle. He thus reduced Jesus' parables to the status of ethical or moral fables.

Clearly, this naive approach could not hold water when we came to apply it to the texts. We soon began to realise the fallacy of this 'go and do thou likewise' understanding, on facing such a parable as the Unjust Steward.[5] This could be no moral tale even if we stood the parable on its head! 'I know we've got to look for the unexpected but I think it would be going too far to believe Jesus was expecting us to go off and go in for fraud like this Unjust Steward. But in the story he is the 'hero', so to speak,' said Ray. Clearly the story was all about being ready for crisis, and simply could not be a moral fable.

The more we looked at parables such as the Seed Growing Secretly, the more we felt that Jesus was not expecting that the coming of the Kingdom would depend upon our own good morals, and yet there was a high moral expectation running through his teaching. Now how could that be reconciled? It seemed to us that any moral imperative which Jülicher had discerned within Jesus' teaching was a call to behave in the way which would be appropriate *in the wake* of the coming of the Kingdom rather than as the necessary forerunner to it. There was a crisis all right but that was because the Kingdom was even now coming into the world. 'So the difference between the parables of Jesus and those of the Old Testament or from science is that his parables are about the Kingdom of God and its immediate arrival', said Jim.

It was good for the group to know that this insight about the parables was confirmed once more by what the scholars had discovered. In 1935, Professor C. H. Dodd had written a book[6] in which he developed the argument that to understand the meaning of Jesus' parables, they must first be placed in their original setting in the ministry of Jesus. He then went on to demonstrate that this setting must have been Jesus' proclamation of the imminent arrival of God's Kingdom as he proclaimed it in Mark 1:15. 'The time is fulfilled, and the Kingdom of God is close at hand. Repent and believe the Gospel.' It was the Kingdom standing over against the prevailing present situation which gave the parables a special place within the teaching and ministry of Jesus. It was this particular dynamic which gave them their function and their confrontational force. In order for us to understand the parables therefore, it now became necessary for us to examine precisely what Jesus was saying in reference to the Kingdom of God.

A. Jesus teaches about the Kingdom of God

'To think of God up in heaven, sitting on his throne and us lot down here not taking a blind bit of notice is a bit like our modern idea of constitutional monarchy, but I don't suppose that's quite what Jesus had in mind?'

Sue was right to suspect that it would not necessarily be a simple matter for us to appreciate the meaning of this 'Kingdom of God' concept. We were tending to think of it as a state of affairs or a place distant from ordinary mortal experience. It all seemed rather abstract, and that did not square well with the picture which was shot through the parable stories. The biblical passages about the Kingdom were much more concrete and spoke, above all else, of God in action rather than sitting and looking on from afar.

So for example in Psalm 146 God is praised for his active Kingly rule in the following terms:

> *Yahweh, forever faithful,*
> *gives justice to those denied it,*
> *gives food to the hungry,*
> *gives liberty to prisoners.*

Yahweh restores sight to the blind,
Yahweh straightens the bent,
Yahweh protects the stranger,
He keeps the orphan and widow.

Yahweh loves the virtuous,
and frustrates the wicked.
Yahweh reigns for ever,
your God, Zion, from age to age.[7]

Our English word 'Kingdom' no longer seemed to us fully to grasp the powerfully active import of the Hebrew concept. In the Bible, God's Kingdom was not simply a matter of God having in his person a latent power, but it was power in action, functioning not as a title or state but as purposeful deed.[8]

'So a Kingdom parable must then have action about it, not just talk', remarked Norah, 'so our name "Parables in Action" makes sense a bit more doesn't it.'

However, as we explored the Old Testament passages which described God's active power we became rather concerned about the constantly recurring theme of God's vengeful and bloodthirsty actions against his enemies. A typical example was to be found in the story of Israel's deliverance from Egypt in Exodus 15:1–12.

I shall sing to Yahweh for he has covered himself in glory,
horse and rider he has thrown into the sea.
. . . You stretched your right hand out, the earth swallowed
them!

The group felt that such language simply didn't square with how they had experienced God themselves. They were intent however, on accepting that God is still locked in battle with evil for in the New Testament we found this was pictured as Jesus' continuing battle against the demons and he is himself reported by Luke to have exclaimed, 'If it is by the finger of God that I cast out demons, then the Kingdom of God has come upon you.'[9] Jesus seems to see his activities as some sort of holy war or conflict between the powers of evil and good, of darkness and light, and there is simply no getting away from the fact that for him the Kingdom inevitably brings conflict. Indeed, the gospel accounts cannot be properly understood without acknowledging the reality of that final conflict on the cross and any interpretation of the parables had to take into account the unquestionable historical certainty that the creator of these parables was crucified for his teaching and activity. So, far from being just lovely children's stories as they're often made out to be, these parables must originally have given such shocking offence that the hearers conspired together to be rid of the creator of them. There had always been of course, within the traditions of the Jewish people, a strong emphasis on prophecy and critique but when a prophet such as Jesus arose, his words and actions were bound to engender hostile reactions from those whose power and influence were thereby threatened.

With this in mind, we could now be more sure that Jülicher had it wrong in suspecting that the parables were in essence only moral fables, because if they had been, then why would Jesus' hearers, who were already moral to the point of obsession, have found any difficulty in them at all? They would have agreed wholeheartedly with moral stories, not gone out of their way to crucify him. Rather, these parables had been used in the cut and thrust of the hotly argued conflict which must have surrounded Jesus and his followers all along. And the reason for this conflict could only have been that as Jesus understood it, the Kingdom of God was totally antagonistic to the ways of the world and the prevailing religiosity of his day. From the Gospel evidence there seemed to be no doubt that if we follow him then we too would have to face up to conflict; and yet we were also noticing that Jesus was constantly promising his disciples not only conflict and crosses to bear, but also an abundance of joy and celebration. One clearly acted sign of this was the way in which the disciples' sharing with Jesus in the hospitality and companionship of the common meal quickly became a very central feature of the life of the New Testament discipleship group. Time and again in the New Testament, Jesus is to be found with his friends at table, and this was in itself an acted symbolic parable which prefigured the great messianic banquet of the Kingdom which had been spoken of so often in the Old Testament.[10] But Jesus stood even this great symbol from the past on its head and he antagonised his Jewish contemporaries by inviting many characters who were beyond the pale in terms of the Jewish Law and expectations to share with him in this symbolic meal. He invited to his Kingdom meal even tax gatherers, sinners and people of bad reputation, so even this foreshadowing of the joy of the Kingdom must have blown the minds of his contemporaries who expected that only the righteous would participate in the joy of the coming messianic age. Jesus invites all to eat in the presence of the all-forgiving Father and thus, even this joyous celebration becomes a frightful challenge and stumbling-block for those who cannot bring themselves to accept the Kingdom in these all-too-generous terms. Everywhere we looked, we found Jesus' teaching and ministry leading him ever into more conflict.

As we brought together what we had learned from these several discussions, we perceived that in Jesus' mind the Kingdom of God was of such a quality that its actions and signs would have to do with God's active power and authority; that it would be in conflict with and in radical opposition to the activities of the Children of Darkness; that it would be a joyous celebration of the very nature of the Godhead; and that it was even now coming into the world.

It was fascinating to sense that there were parallels here between how Jesus had created his parables and parabolic actions and what had happened to us in our little Parables in Action group. Like him, we too had become aware of the conflict between what we saw in our surroundings and what we sensed the Kingdom of God to demand. We too had now learned that the dynamics of Kingdom activity always stand over against the darkness of this present age, and that the parables were designed to bring this tension to the consciousness of the hearers amidst the conflict. This is how the parables were used by Jesus and it was our hope too that our Community Advice Centre would be a small parabolic light in the present urban darkness.

B. Jesus shatters old illusions

We were now convinced that the parables are, along with other elements in Jesus' ministry, signs of God's active presence in the world – in other words, they are Signs of the Kingdom. With this in mind, our Parables in Action group took time to list many of the actions of Jesus recorded in the Gospels and drew from each what they signified for us about the Kingdom. We drew up a chart, similar to that which we had used for our God's Unexpected session, entering in on one side the stories from Jesus' ministry, and on the other side what it was about the Kingdom which each signified. In some healings, as for example of the woman with a haemorrhage,[11] it seemed to us that a person who is normally unnoticed becomes noticed, so the sign being pointed up here was that the non-celebrities become celebrated in the Kingdom. When a leper is healed[12] it is a sign that outcasts and marginalised people are welcomed by the Kingdom activity. With the healing of the Syro-Phoenician women's daughter[13] comes the sign that in the Kingdom barriers of ethnicity and gender are torn down. When disciples pick corn on the Sabbath it tells us that in the Kingdom the accepted authorities are challenged.[14] As Jesus broke bread and poured wine, so those engaged in Kingdom activity see that in their joy they must also suffer.[15]

And so we continued until Marjorie interjected, 'These Signs of the Kingdom are just like God's Unexpected but now I'm finding it a lot easier to see it now that we've had more experience working out and preparing for our project. When we first looked at God's Unexpected, I found it really difficult but now I'm beginning to get the hang of it. I wonder if that's because we've been praying about it properly now and before our prayers were bland. It takes a lot of hard work to keep our imagination broad enough to compare what we usually expect with what the Kingdom expects, but it's coming!'

When we compare God's Kingdom activity with the activity of 'this world order' then the bankruptcy of our own activity, structures and concerns becomes all too clear. It is only then that it becomes easy to realise why Jesus met with such profound antagonism and enmity. But he pushed his point again and again, apparently so that the polarisation between this world's values and the Kingdom of God would be brought into much sharper focus such that a response was demanded by the new clarity. Now that the *need* for this polarisation was better understood in our group, it became possible to understand what Jesus was getting at when he was asked what the parables were supposed to do. He replied 'everything comes in parables *so that* they may look and look, but never perceive; listen and listen, but never understand; to avoid changing their ways and being healed.'[16] Alienation has to be focused before it can be purged.[17] Jesus' statement in the words and actions of the Kingdom alternative is a new present reality which calls the 'normal' to account. The experience of those who see the signs or listen to the parables is the experience of the confronted. It is a time of testing and crisis for it becomes a time for decision and for decisive action. The parable or Kingdom Sign places the hearers at a new crossroads and calls them to participate in or be judged by the action it symbolises.[18]

When Jesus proclaimed his Kingdom he spoke of good news to the poor, liberty to captives, sight for the blind, freedom for the downtrodden and a Jubilee to be celebrated.[19] We were setting up the Community Advice Centre hoping thereby to embody a Sign of this Kingdom over against what we perceived to be an offensive state of affairs in our locality. Like Jesus' parables, it was in this sense confrontational and like Kuhn's paradigms it was already producing new insights by virtue of the new way we now had of looking at things. We now felt ourselves to be in a different place from when we started out on our project. We had learnt a lot since we started and made many big decisions for ourselves. We had actually done things we'd never have thought we could have done. The Advice Centre had not even opened yet but already we felt that we had come a long way.

It seemed that we were beginning to realise that things had been happening to us that we had not appreciated and perhaps that was because as well as being directly confrontational, the parable has another, strangely subtle quality.

Before we had begun our research into the locality, we had
been under the odd illusion that there were no great problems
in our society, but it was precisely such lack of insight which
our acted parable was beginning to rectify. We had not been
accurately reading the Signs of the Kingdom, but neither
had we been reading the signs of the times! But now, by
virtue of all that we'd had to do so far, our acted parable was
beginning to get under the skin of these old illusions, almost
without us realising it. 'Now why was this?' we asked
ourselves. When Kierkegaard was considering the nature of
illusions, he had come to the conclusion that 'a direct attack
only strengthens a person in his illusion and at the same time
embitters him. There is nothing that requires such gentle
handling as an illusion, if one wishes to dispel it.'(20) We felt
that we had been somewhat taken off our guard and our old
illusions about our society and our area had been dispelled,
although we had not been aware of it happening.

'We used to believe that no-one need really be poor in
Britain today but now we've seen the evidence and we know
that's rubbish. The project has made us look properly for
the first time', announced Sue.

'We thought it was true, like everyone else', Colin
protested, 'and we thought that if anyone was poor it was
their own fault; but now we've had to learn that the truth is
very different. It's just like the prophets of the Old Testament. Like Nathan who told that nice gentle story to King
David, got him relaxed and interested in the story, before
homing in on the real point.'

What the parable was able to do, it seemed to us, was to
keep the listeners and their illusions spell-bound and only
then did the sting come in its tail. So when Jesus is asked
why he used parable stories, he could very well have replied
'No one can enter a strong man's house and plunder his
goods unless he first binds the strong man; then indeed he
may plunder his house.'(21) The fascination of the parable
story, and the fascination of the Advice Centre activity, had
the power to spell-bind the strong man so that his defences
were dropped. We had been enticed into dropping our guard
so that the parable could confront whilst at the same time
giving us a new opportunity, a newly presented choice.

'I think I'm beginning to get the hang of the parables at last', Sue proclaimed. 'They're really quite subversive, aren't they?'

C. Sharing our hopes

It was clear to us that we still had very much to learn, but we felt that we had already come so very far together along our journey of faith and commitment that we genuinely had much to celebrate and for which to give thanks. We felt that the time had come to design one of our Sunday worship services specifically around the theme of our project and to thank God for what had so far taken place. We wanted to ask Him also to bless us on our way by making our project participate even more overtly in his Kingdom activity. During this great eucharistic service, all those who were in any way involved in the project stood for their commissioning. Firstly, a time of silence was kept to consider the seriousness of the moment. Then the words of the Commission were read:

You have been called by God to a new task.
You have been called by God to participate in the new Community Advice Centre here in this community, that it may be a sign of God's love for us and for all people.
Do you then promise to do your utmost to serve Christ in your neighbour in this place?
Do you promise to help the project by giving your talents and your time; by offering yourself for training, and sharing with all those in need?

All replied: We do, God being our helper.

May you be strengthened by God to do his will and may you be richly rewarded by seeing Signs of His Kingdom.

To be present at the service was a very moving experience, as many commented later. For those who had not heard of the project before, it informed clearly and directly. They said how they felt it had been openly shared with them and in

some way they too had been touched by its meaning. For
those of us who had been close to the project for a long while,
the service was a time of faithfulness. God's faithfulness to
His promise was manifest, and our response of commitment
was worshipfully presented for His will to be done. Our own
sense of discipleship was undoubtedly heightened and our
sense of responsibility to God and the community deepened.
We shared grave doubts about our own adequacy for the task
and it was this service of commissioning which gave us the
further faith and resolve, knowing in whose service we
shared.

On the evening before the Centre was due to open, the
Parables in Action group, in relaxed style, did a very simple
ground-clearing exercise. We drew a large chart, similar in
design to a Rugby football goal or capital letter H. The left
hand upright was representative of where we were now, the
right hand upright of where we would be in one year's time.
Above the horizontal 'cross-bar' were our 'best hopes' and
below, our 'worst fears'. At each of the four corners of the
diagram, we were to write what we now felt. As our off-the-
cuff answers occurred to our group, so we wrote them up on
our chart.[22]

What did we feel we now had in our project that we would
not like to see disappear? These positive factors we wrote up
in the top left corner. First and foremost, we were thankful
to acknowledge that thus far we had been led by what the
biblical mandates had taught us – Christianity in action and
real commitment. We could write up too that we had money
secured for the project to function efficiently. We had
welcoming premises. Already we had some expertise. We
had planned very carefully and were thankful for that. We
had outside support from various agencies. We had a definite
team spirit which was not exclusive. We felt the presence of
the Holy Spirit with us and finally – we had Christian hope!

We looked at the lower end of the upright. Here we had
to name those things which we were presently not happy
about. What we did *not* have, which we particularly felt the
lack of, was experience. Confidence too at this stage was a
little shaky. We needed some more communication with our

Our Hopes & Fears Diagram

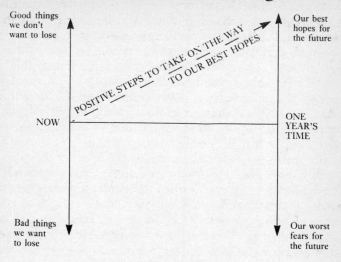

Good things
we don't
want to lose

POSITIVE STEPS TO TAKE ON THE WAY
TO OUR BEST HOPES

Our best
hopes for
the future

NOW

ONE
YEAR'S
TIME

Bad things
we want
to lose

Our worst
fears for
the future

community and time for real trust to grow and flourish. We also knew that there were bound to be some who could not accept help amongst our community and acknowledged that that could perfectly well be our own fault as a church.

The strangely relaxed mood allowed us to discuss quite freely our present strengths and weaknesses and also to look ahead at what could possibly go wrong in the future. What were our nightmares? We wrote them at the bottom right of our diagram. Perhaps our team would just dissolve and that could happen for any number of reasons. Perhaps disillusionment would set in and our commitment and enthusiasm would wane. Perhaps no support would be forthcoming, or perhaps, worst of all, an élitism could grow up within the project which would counter all that we had hoped to achieve.

But, finally we could be positive and list on our chart all the best things that we could hope for in one year's time. It would be too optimistic to hope that society would be in no more need of a Community Advice Centre project, but it was worth noting, to remind ourselves that our project after all was a means to an end and not an end in itself! More realistically, we hoped to have accrued more experience and confidence, to have learnt more patience and faith, and by being more at one with our community, to have much greater knowledge of its needs and resources, its issues and concerns. We hoped that the project would teach us more about ourselves and our fellowship, and most important, that it might be a parable of the Kingdom activity of God.

Having thus clarified our overall aims and fears, it now became possible to draw a further line on our diagram running from the midpoint of where we now were, up to join our best hopes for the future. Along this line, we listed all the clear and concrete steps we could take in order to achieve our best hopes. These clear-cut objectives derived from what we had already said we wanted to achieve and what we wanted to avoid, and included such things as 'build in constant theological reflection', 'honest prayer', 'in-service training', 'welcome all-comers', 'be prepared to critique one-another', 'keep searching for fresh biblical insight', and 'use the common-sense of the community'.

We sat quietly together. We felt very close, with a gentle sense of anticipation and excitement. We seemed to have been brought a long way together and had been empowered to do things of which many of us would previously have felt incapable. We sensed a deep solidarity in our discipleship and looked to the future with wide-open expectations. What a very new experience that was for so many of the group.

5: Action and Reflection

A. The first days

After fourteen months of careful reflection and detailed planning the doors of the Community Advice Centre officially opened at two o'clock on 11th February 1981. The Centre entrance area acted as a very welcoming reception room. Colourful posters were displayed everywhere giving information about the community and the church. Magazines and leaflets were available free from a display cabinet, giving advice on legal aid, social security benefits and the like. Through the glass doors to the right could be seen the church sanctuary and to the left was the kitchen from which tea and coffee were always available. Comfortable chairs and low tables were all around the carpeted area to help promote a relaxed atmosphere. A number of rooms leading off from the entrance area were available as we needed them. On that important day there was a great deal of activity in and around the room which acted as the office and this gave every impression of an effective and busy session. In fact, all that was happening was that the parish magazine was being typed and cabinets being moved around the office to create more space. No-one visited the Centre and the Day Book received no entries! What a dreadful disappointment that was. We had been warned that there would inevitably be a slow take-up before the community's trust in the Centre was established but, after so much anticipation, it was a disappointment nevertheless. Even so, there was still much to be done in the office because the Information Pack had constantly to be updated and local information had to be collated.

We were so clearly aware of our own lack of experience

that we had been getting into the habit, during the preceding weeks, of meeting at the Centre at the proposed times of opening, to try to establish a routine and a team spirit. We were, strangely, somewhat relieved that the first session passed without event because we were anxious to gain experience slowly and steadily and would have been overwhelmed if too many had come on the first day. To some extent, the lack of take-up was deliberate policy on our part because we had decided to keep our advertising, in the initial stages at least, quite minimal and local, and only to enlarge it as we developed our resources and skill. A very brief account of our intention to open a Community Advice Centre had appeared some months before in the local newspaper, and in early February a duplicated paper was given to our own Church members which briefly stated the hours of opening, gave the telephone number and indicated that the service was free and confidential. It seemed somewhat extraordinary to us therefore, that when our doors opened for our evening session that same February day, there stood our first customer and he had heard the news in a public house on the other side of the city! A telephone enquiry followed from an Irish family who had only just arrived in Birmingham to escape the 'troubles' in Belfast, and with that we realised that it was not entirely in our hands to determine just how many people were going to get to know about our project.

Despite some busy moments, it was to remain true that the take-up in the service was very slow at first and there would sometimes be two or three sessions together without a single enquiry. To begin with, it was truly a relief, and yet clearly there was a growing need for our advertising to be built up. Bright yellow posters with a handshake design and the motto 'Share a trouble – halve a problem', were displayed in strategic shop windows, pubs, doctors' waiting rooms, launderettes, the Community Centre and other such places in the community. Whenever a local event drew people together, such as church getherings, jumble sales or the Erdington Carnival, our members were handing cards round to families and bystanders and whenever a card was given, a word of greeting and explanation went with it. Even so, this coverage was limited in order that we would not be overwhelmed by too many enquiries.

B. Gaining experience

As we met week by week and as we discussed matters at workers' meetings and in the Parables in Action group, so we began to find a common mind and spirit. But we all had much to learn. In those early weeks, team members would stand around the office chatting nervously or just looking rather lost until firmly reminded to utilise their time well and read and acquaint themselves further with the files of information. One by one, each adviser broke their duck and worked with a visitor on an issue. Usually on their first such occasion, all the training they had received was forgotten and the adviser would rush into the office for a file of information on the relevant subject, looking very flustered and not really in full possession of the facts of the case at all. Repeatedly the same assertion was made, 'Thank goodness we're not overwhelmed with visitors yet, or we would all be in a flat spin.'

One of our first inquiries involved a woman who had run away from her violent husband, had now found accommodation but had no furniture. After the initial inevitable panic, the team settled into working alongside the woman and her children in giving her the contacts she needed. That evening we were unloading a bed for the children, and the other basic requirements of furniture, from a borrowed van into her local home. Another 'phone enquiry from a young woman, was seeking accommodation for a family who apparently had been treated badly when they applied to the city housing authorities. We were able to supply lists of helpful addresses and contacts, and assured her that we would go into it all in more detail if she were able to attend the Centre in person, because she was obviously not used to using the telephone and was getting very muddled and overwhelmed by it.

It was a very humbling experience when only the next week these two women contacted the Centre again to tell us that when they had initially come to us they had all but given up hope. Now they felt so much more positive and indeed were beginning to make real headway in the issue they had to face. They thanked us profusely and told us how much more human and caring their experience at our Centre had been than with the authorised but rather bureaucratic agencies. We knew that we had helped in only very small ways and yet now we felt even more convinced of the worthwhileness of the project.

The receptionists were keeping the atmosphere in the Centre very welcoming and homely, so that as time went on, if visitors had to wait on a busy day, the receptionists would befriend them and help them relax. Very often, if the adviser had to apologise for keeping a visitor waiting, the visitor would reply 'Oh, that's all right, I've had a lovely chat with this lady and a nice cup of tea'. On Advice Centre evenings the church entrance area could at times become full of happy chatter, for very often visitors would come as a family, would recognise a receptionist as a local friend and sit chatting freely about the difficulty for some time before speaking with an adviser or solicitor. Since other parts of the church building were also used on these evenings, people who had come for reasons other than to visit the Community Advice Centre, would congregate for a cup of tea and a chat and this helped to enhance the warm atmosphere.

But it took a very long time for numbers to build up and it is true to say of our earliest days that the number actually attending at the Centre with problems to be faced were few, especially during afternoon sessions. We used this time to reflect carefully in our Parables in Action group upon what we were learning and we made changes accordingly. We could see, for example, that it was important that the adviser and visitor should be aware that they were equals, sharing information, and that no visitor should be given the impression that we knew the answers to their life's problems and they did not. The visitor then was never given false impressions about our standing or expertise. We were, as they, searching for an answer to common problems.

Enthusiasm certainly was not waning despite the feeling on occasions that we spent more time waiting than serving.

During such time we were gaining more understanding one of another and sharing our learning as we gained experience. Because few enquiries were being worked at, each was being considered carefully and where mistakes were made, steps were taken to note them and learn from them.

But as our confidence increased, so our frustration at the length of time spent just waiting for visitors to come to the Centre became more aggravating. The more experience we gained, the better became the service we could offer and yet the service was not being taken up as we had hoped. Some of our team were beginning to voice a certain amount of frustration in these early days even though they had been warned to expect a very slow take-up of the service. This experience of having to wait was, we noted, akin to the feelings of frustration and powerlessness being voiced by many who attended as visitors to the Centre. They felt worthless and powerless to act in the face of problems which confronted them and we felt rather unused and disregarded too. It was only through careful reflection upon these initial feelings of uselessness and powerlessness that we gained valuable and fascinating theological insights which will be related later after we have described what happened next at the Centre.

C. Confronting the issues?

As the weeks went by, as our advertising was noticed and as the word got around the neighbourhood, so the numbers attending at the Community Advice Centre increased. Whilst still within manageable bounds, this increase dissipated any sense of frustration amongst the team as they continued to gain experience in working with our visitors. Numbers of volunteers increased to twenty in all and many of those who had begun as receptionists went forward for basic training in advice work.

As we had expected, many visitors were facing difficulties in relation to government departments and statutory agencies. The bureaucratic nature of large departments had often alienated our visitors. Mrs B. had complained of the unhealthy state of her accommodation so often to the Housing Department without success, that when we put pressure on to have a plumber visit her house to improve the sanitation, she sent him away 'with a good telling-off' for not having come before. She returned to the Centre apologetically, unable to understand how she could have done such a negative thing just when some success was on the horizon. But this was a common experience amongst our visitors. Often massive rent arrears were allowed to build up in order to spite the council for having neglected the properties for so long. But of course this quite understandable policy of non-payment had only served to reinforce the vicious circle of antagonism so that deadlock and mistrust pervaded every avenue of enquiry.

Families felt themselves very much at the mercy of the official rule book. One woman had saved sufficient money to buy a ticket to Ireland to visit her dying father but no advance discretionary payment from the Welfare system was available to help her to live for a week or two once she had arrived there. It seemed that the rule was that no payments were made in advance. We could see every reason for the ruling but as we sat with the woman, we also shared in her feeling of despair at her plight. So often our experience put us in this powerless situation alongside our visitors. Sometimes our information system itself proved inadequate and a pamphlet or information brochure would be missing or out of print just when we needed it. We had the wherewithal to inquire further but for the time being we had to share their frustration at just not having the information to hand on which a decision could be made. We were also often baffled ourselves by the complex forms and cryptic information which the government departments published. Explanatory government forms were sometimes found to be self-contradictory, so we would 'phone for an explanation, and merely be referred back to the same unintelligible pamphlet for an answer. If we, as a trained team, could not translate the information into plain English, then how could an untrained enquirer be expected to understand it? And how was a non-English speaking visitor to cope? With regard to the latter case, we were pleased to have offers of assistance in translation of Asian languages, and it was not long in any case before a Punjabi-speaking Hindu joined the team.

In many cases, a visitor would attend the Centre with a direct request for information and it would be possible to give it. Sometimes, it was clear that the visitors were far more *au fait* with the system or problem than we were, and they helped us to interpret the information or the tables of figures. It was very encouraging when sometimes we found that the visitor was entitled to provision or redress and on following up the case was given help and encouragement by the appropriate official. In some respects we found that the avenues and structures of the State worked amazingly well and were staffed by caring and hard-working officials. There was no doubt that some were heavily prejudiced and bitterly patronising, but others were genuinely seeking to be of real service.[1]

What came home to us most clearly was that most of our visitors lived in a totally different culture from that which seemed to be demanded by the official structures. The State would service most enquirers, but the channels of relationship and negotiation were bureaucratic and official. If the enquirer made application in a servile and orthodox manner and preferably in writing, then the chances of success, if the application was seen to be justified, were reasonably high. The service which such an applicant would receive would be courteous and civil, considering the ridiculously large workload with which each officer, often untrained, was expected to cope. If however, a family was in such a situation as not to be able to follow these required strategies, then things did not go so well and indeed antagonism could easily mount up and things could soon become offensive and bitter. This could arise out of simple misunderstanding, as when Mrs K. had requested of the court that since she was paying a heavy fine for her son who had stolen property, then it was her right to keep that property since she now felt that in effect she had paid for it. When a scene therefore flared up in court, Mrs K. was so upset and angry that she even failed to realise that a Court Order was simultaneously being made to take her son from her and put him into care. When this was explained to her after the hearing, she was distraught.

Mrs K. came regularly to the Centre for comfort and some explanation. Not even her own legal counsel had taken the time to make sure that what he had explained to Mrs K. had been rightly heard and understood.

Very often, this total breakdown in communication was at the heart of real distress. Many elderly pensioners came to the Centre with anxiety over simple matters which were soon dissipated when carefully explained in language they could understand, by people who had taken the trouble to investigate where the misunderstandings were arising. This constant failure of communication was aggravated by the anxiety it could so easily cause. A visitor might come, for example, worried that a prison sentence would be forthcoming since it appeared that he or she had failed to obey the rules. Once the fear of any such punishment was lifted, then it became more possible for the visitor to behave normally once again. Only rarely did official or government agencies show sufficient respect for their 'clients' to make sure that things were clearly and sensitively explained and so this task of interpretation was a constant feature of the Centre's work. It was not always fair however to blame the individuals working for the agency for the administrative straight-jacket that they were in. It seemed rather that the system demanded a certain methodology and procedure and had little or no flexibility to account for the human predicaments which it had been designed to serve. We noted repeatedly too that the local offices of the helping agencies, such as the DHSS, could be so demeaning and inhuman that some visitors could just not cope with the humiliation of attending there.

Perhaps we met with the most subtle frustration of all when we achieved success. The S. family came to us in great distress. They desperately needed to move from their present accommodation. They had no rent arrears owing, the mother was ill and needed to move to a less hilly area near shops and preferably near her daughter some five miles distant. She was not only partially deaf, but also had difficulty in coming to terms with the complexities of the officialdom with which she had met whenever she had applied for transfer. We were able to write to the Housing Department on her behalf and later chase up this application for a move. We underlined the importance of the case and helped to interpret each side to the other. How very pleased we were when we heard that at last the S. family had been offered, and had accepted, accommodation quite near the daughter's house. We felt a real sense of achievement that our hard work had met with success and we even wrote a letter of thanks to the Housing Department for their help in the matter. But deep in our hearts we knew that our pressure had helped Mrs S. to the front of a very long queue of families in our city who are in similar circumstances but with no-one to plead for them. Were we helping to solve a problem or were we helping our friends to jump queues?[2]

In other cases, matters were not so ambiguous. The Day Book sometimes had to record in the 'Action Taken' column: 'Really nothing we can do except listen'. A mother with vast rent arrears owing, heavily in debt, with sons in care and daughter prostituting, neighbour problems and housing in dangerous disrepair, still visits the Centre quite often. Perhaps she comes for a quiet break, a cup of tea and a cigarette. There seems little more we can do. Alan double-checked her Social Security entitlement and managed to get it slightly increased but the neighbours continue to bother her and with money still owing there is little in the near future which can really put some sparkle back into her life. And yet, as we all chat together, she raises a smile and we get the feeling that here she feels amongst friends. We share her powerlessness over a cup of tea. We know that, given a steady and improved income, she would have the wherewithal and prudence to get the family into better shape, but present financial conditions preclude any such hope.

It was not only in the Centre or during the set opening hours that work was undertaken. Although limited by our experience and resources a great deal of follow-up work took place even in these earliest months. Already having contacts in the community meant that it was possible quickly to organise visiting where it was necessary – elderly folk soon had their gardens tidied up for them by willing youngsters; essential furniture was hustled and delivered; run-away children were searched for (and run-away cars for that matter!)

Handicapped people who could not get to the Centre were visited by our team and whenever a referral was obviously necessary this was done as sensitively as possible. Sometimes our follow-up services would be continued over a long period, as for example when we acted as cashier for Valerie and Michael. They had got themselves heavily in debt and could only save up what they owed by bringing two pounds a week to the Centre for us to lock away for them in the church safe. In this way their arrears and debts were very slowly paid off.

Madeleine led a fine team of workers and her own commitment and devotion to the needs of all those who visited or made enquiries by 'phone was an inspiration to all. She had a gentle style but made sure that there was an excellence and precision about the work. It was not always easy to know however how best to respond to the enquiries and we were not always very sure as to what to do for the best. Sometimes we grew anxious that we had not seen a visitor for some weeks when we knew they really were still in trouble. If we knew that we were in a position to do something to alleviate the situation, the problem we had to face was whether it would really be helpful by burdening them with ourselves, or indeed to know when we were just not wanted. It did occur to us that perhaps a good servant should only come when called and for us to poke our noses in could be a dominating act and not a serving one. This was a real dilemma. Additionally, there were the natural human failings on our side when perhaps we had failed fully to understand a visitor's situation or had not been able to locate information quickly enough.

But perhaps our most dangerous failing was our continuing prejudice. Sometimes our prejudice would be levelled against a government official who, on reflection, really had been doing his or her very best, given the limitations under which they had to work. Sometimes a prejudice against a visitor seemed to have some justification, but occasionally a more unwarranted comment would be heard from team members as they discussed a case at a Workers' Meeting. It was markedly evident however that such lapses became few and far between as our experience grew and as we became more aware of the implications of people's real plight. Our practical work experience was clearly raising our political and theological consciousness.

As the project went forward, so experience accumulated and a great deal was learnt from day-to-day activity at the Community Advice Centre. There was much to celebrate, for certain breakthroughs had encouraged us. Conversely, there were certain disappointments which we found frustrating. We had opportunity to come to terms with both our positive and negative experiences in the reflective meetings which the Parables in Action group continued to run.

D. Teasing out the themes

We had moved from initial reflection upon our local situation into action. Now that our project was operative, it was our intention to embark upon action-based reflection once again and to continue to consider theologically what our acted parable, the Community Advice Centre, was teaching us. Thus we were forming a circle of action, reflection, action and reflection.

We found that we were most productive if we ran our theology workshops in series of about ten weekly meetings followed by a rest period of about a month. We met in the evenings, people arriving in twos and threes to avoid the dangers of the dark back streets. Sometimes we met in the church meeting room and at other times in the houses of group members. On occasion we would begin with an informal eucharist but usually we would get straight down to working on the issue in which we were engaged. The group members would tend to be meeting for other purposes during the week too, be it for socials, outings, clubs and so on, and our discussions would often spill over into these more informal gatherings. But the real work went on when we met up as the Parables in Action group.

So it was that the next series of meetings of that group looked carefully at the experience of the early months of work at the Community Advice Centre to see if this acted

parable was presenting any themes which could propel us
into more critical consciousness. Because we knew one
another well there was very little reluctance to participate,
and we listened very carefully to those who were personally
involved in the advice work. They told us that at first they
had had a genuine fear of their own inadequacy and inability
to come up to the expectation of visitors who would perhaps
have expected them to be professionals. After only a very
short time, however, this feeling of inadequacy and fear of
the unknown had turned to frustration because although the
Advice Centre seemed to us to be a weapon in the fight
against what was weighing people down, it was not being
given a chance to operate to full effect. People were simply
not turning up and numbers were down to what seemed like
a pathetic trickle. Workers felt they were wasting time in
the afternoon sessions particularly, just sitting and waiting
around. We began to conjure with feeble excuses; maybe our
position in the road was wrong, or perhaps the advertising
should have been earlier after all. Marjorie reminded us that
in some senses it was a real relief that we were not being
pressed by too many visitors for this had given the workers
time to sort themselves out before the rush came. But Ray
was concerned because having to wait like this was frustrating
the purpose. The word which was constantly coming forward,
which was being used first positively and then negatively, was
the simple but central word 'waiting'. We were all waiting
for an increased use of the Centre; we were feeling that our
waiting was sometimes simply wasting time; we were using
some of our waiting time in preparation; sometimes we were
waiting like a spare-part on a shelf; sometimes our feeling
of anxiety and inadequacy as we waited could be likened to
the feelings of powerlessness that our visitors must have been
having constantly. And underlying all this waiting was an
anxiety about what the future might hold.

Perhaps at this early stage the issue was not absolutely
clear in our minds but we felt that this 'waiting' might be a
theme word which would focus our experience well and prove
to be a way into the central issue for us. We took this
word and determined to look at different aspects of it at the
forthcoming meetings. Because at the Community Advice

Centre we were alongside some folk who were made to stand in some senses aside from any proper participation in society we felt that to start off our reflection we should begin by thinking together about those who are waiting in this way – on the margins of life.

E. Waiting on the margins

The next week as we met, on the wall where our charts, diagrams and sketches were displayed, were hung two pictures. The first was of elderly, lonely men sitting silently in a cafe at separate tables, just waiting. We thought of that line in Ralph McTell's song, 'Each tea lasts an hour and he wanders home alone.'[3]

'We often have people coming to the Centre who otherwise would have no-one at all in their lives. Imagine it!' said Beryl.

The other picture portrayed women patients in a geriatric ward. They sat there waiting, on the fringes of life, disabled by ailing bodies and minds. They were left there by society and forced to its margins because they no longer seemed 'useful'. The black members of our group were able to recount stories of the British society pushing them to its margins but it was not because of any such myth about being of no use, quite the contrary. In the 'fifties and 'sixties British industry and government had recruited Caribbean people to the UK precisely because of their usefulness to the thriving industry of a booming society. They told us how they came expecting to be welcomed by a mother country and a mother church but instead were spat at in the street, were herded into abysmal and crowded accommodation and made to work as stereotyped manual labour for very low wages. Bob told us how he and his friends would save all their money to buy the cheapest of suits so that they could send pictures home which gave at least an impression that they had been properly received in Britain and that they were happy. Rarely would they tell their parents and cousins back home how cruel the reality was. They had dutifully attended the Anglican and Methodist churches until they couldn't stand the cold shoulders any longer. It was amazing that so many put up with it

for so long. In fact even today after such treatment black
people continue to number nearly ten per cent of all worship-
ping Anglicans in Birmingham.[4]

'Coming to a strange country as a youngster was bad
enough but when you've been told that you'll be welcomed
and then you meet such racism, you really do feel you've
been pushed to the margins', Louise confided. The black
generation that has grown up since, has never known life in
the Caribbean but has experienced the economic decline
of Europe. The racist marginalisation for them has been
compounded by unemployment and all the usual deprivation
of the urban scene where so many of them have been ghet-
toed. The younger black generations sit and wait. 'But I
don't think they're going to wait much longer!' said Bob.

The room was soon buzzing as different group members
recounted their experience of marginalisation. Jack had
recently suffered a stroke and had felt the severe frustration
because, now semi-paralysed and only able to speak with
great difficulty, he had when healthy been a very outgoing
and energetic person. Jack managed a few powerful phrases:
'loneliness but quietness – been a revelation – lots to learn –
build up carefully – slowly, very slowly.'

The frustration of waiting can sometimes be felt most
keenly in the rebuff one feels at not being allowed to do what
one feels gifted for or cut out to do.

'You can no longer affirm yourself', interposed Sue who,
since the birth six years ago of her second child, had been
deaf in one ear. 'It cuts you off so from being in touch with
the action. You feel such a fool; straining away to pick up
just snatches of conversation and people think you're stupid
because they haven't realised you just haven't heard them.
Unless you can learn patience, you can suffer a lot, I can tell
you.'[5]

One of the group had brought to the meeting a newspaper
cutting that had appeared in a national daily the week before.
The story was of a man who had artificial legs and walked
with crutches. He also had a disabled wife to care for. On
attending at his city council offices he was told that to apply
for any special allowances he would need to visit the office
on the top floor. Unfortunately, the lift was out of order and

so he was obliged to crawl up the stairs to the office. When he at last arrived, he was told by the officer that, since he was obviously fit enough to get to this top floor, he was not sufficiently disabled to warrant any special allowances! It seemed very difficult to understand how the patience of which Sue had spoken could be of much solace to those in such oppressed circumstances. Was it right to expect people to accept these situations? Should they just sit and wait? Surely the Gospel mandate against such injustice was crystal clear.

There was certainly no doubt in our minds that the marginalised person often has very much to teach others about life. It seemed that here we had struck upon a typical Gospel reversal of all that the world expects – or as we had called it earlier, an example of God's Unexpected. There had been a recent appearance on television of a spastic lawyer of great ability. He had hardly any control over his body and had only learnt to speak with great difficulty. He had become chief librarian of the legal department of a famous company. The interviewer asked him what wish he would choose if it could be granted. He replied that he would wave his magic wand to make everybody 'handicapped'. Then after a few months he would wave it again to return all people to their former state. We viewers had jumped to the conclusion that this ploy was designed to teach the able-bodied just how horrific a life of disablement would be. The lawyer answered differently – 'It would make the able-bodied realise just how much the disabled know about life and just how much the able-bodied have to learn from us!'

'You know it's similar with us black folk,' added Sylvy. 'It's good to hear folk say that I'm black; if they can't see that they must be blind, goodness knows! But I want to be treated as a person – not just as 'one of those'. The thing that hurts me most is when white folk at work treat you as if you had no intelligence. They're having a discussion and if you put your point of view they look at you as if you couldn't have an opinion in your head!' Sylvy was opposed to the use of categories to depersonalise people but she had also drawn the important distinction between respecting and ignoring essential elements in a person's uniqueness. The white liberal pretence that 'we're all the same really' was another clever way of ignoring what we all have to learn from the black experience.

With this insight in mind, Emma drew our attention to some biblical stories which seemed so relevant. We studied a very interesting passage recorded in Mark's and Matthew's gospels[6] where Jesus shows very great reluctance to have anything to do with a woman from a so-called inferior race; after all he is a Jew and she a Syro-Phoenician. She pleads with him to heal her daughter but Jesus does not even answer her. Eventually, he rather insults her origins – 'It is not fair to take the children's food and throw it to the little dogs.' But she replies by pointing out that even if she were a 'little dog' she still has much to share with Jesus even from her demeaned position and inferior status. Her retort is such as to awaken Jesus to new creative insight and he receives her in granting her request.

'She's very persistent and when she shows him her humanity, he has to give in. If only we would give in and see the humanity of those who are being hurt! If Jesus is prepared to learn something from her, then surely we can't be so high and mighty as not to listen', said Marjorie.

We had become shrewdly aware from our reflections that evening that we, the Church, must stop and listen to what those on the margins have to teach us.[7] Perhaps then we would begin to perceive that those oppressed people in reality were not at life's margins but, as Jesus saw, right at its very heart. If we could just stop talking and wait and listen then our waiting might be of real service.

F. Ageism – waiting years

Very many of those who attended at the Community Advice Centre were elderly and they often experienced acute anxiety about problems arising from such things as pension books, wills, health, security and rent payments. Age brings with it particular burdens just as youth brings its own array of challenges; yet our society goes to the extreme in categorising its members by age and gears its ratio of care to those most useful to its productive forces. The young feel that they are waiting to grow up and be useful wage earners and thus hope to receive the freedom they crave; the elderly can sometimes be set aside from 'useful society' and made to feel that they can only sit and wait for death. They are not treated as real persons any longer by our fast-moving society. It's either life in the fast lane or you're parked in a boring lay-by.

Edna had been studying a book about the elderly's experience of life in our society and in it she had found a poem which she introduced and read to us. It had been found in the locker of Kate, an elderly hospital patient who before her death had been unable to speak but occasionally had been seen to write.

What do you see nurses? What do you see?
Are you thinking when you are looking at me
A crabbit old woman not very wise,
Uncertain of habit with far-away eyes,
Who dribbles her food and makes no reply,
When you say in a loud voice 'I do wish you'd try'
Who seems not to notice the things that you do,
And forever is losing a stocking or shoe,
Who unresisting or not lets you do as you will
With bathing and feeding the long day to fill,
Is that what you're thinking, is that what you see?
Then open your eyes nurse. You're not looking at me . . .
I'm an old woman now and nature is cruel,
'Tis her jest to make old age look like a fool.
The body it crumbles, grace and vigour depart,
There now is a stone where I once had a heart:
But inside this old carcase a young girl still dwells,
And now and again my battered heart swells,
I remember the joys, I remember the pain,
And I'm loving and living life over again,
I think of the years all too few – gone too fast,
And accept the stark fact that nothing can last.
So open your eyes nurses, open and see,
Not a crabbit old woman, look closer – see ME.[8]

We looked silently at one another after hearing Kate's poem

and mused upon how many in our society share her experience of being pushed to one side. Emily looked indignant as she spoke:

'We used to go and visit old Mrs D. in that home. I've never seen anything like it in all my life. Just two of them happily chatting and the rest looking like waxworks. It's a most dreadful sight. Just sitting there waiting for something – or nothing. They're just fed and looked after – there's no reason. We used to say, "Can't they have hosts and hostesses?" and the nurses would say that they liked it better that way. It didn't used to be like that when we were kids. There was always Gran' or Grandad in the corner of every kitchen – oh, the kids used to play them up I must admit. Sometimes of course the old folk would rule the bloomin' place an' all – the young had to learn a bit of patience – but either way the elderly weren't shut away before they really had to have special treatment.'

At the other extreme, even childhood is a comparatively recent phenomenon, historically speaking. As we looked at some prints of medieval paintings, the children there didn't seem to be 'children' in our modern sense but merely small people in adult clothes doing adult jobs looking like manikin figures. Even into the early industrial period, as soon as children were physically strong enough they became productive members of the family in every way – very different from today. The great increase in the speed of technological change today could to some degree account for the separation of the generations and the breakdown of mutual respect at that level.

'Once you could ask Grandad about your apprenticeship skills,' said Fred, 'and he would help because the family had been in the same trade for generations and the skills had not changed all that much. But today if a young boy asked his father about the computer or the lathe which he now operates his father wouldn't have a clue! That sort of thing diminishes mutual respect between generations.'

In the agricultural community of St. Kitts and Jamaica where some of our members had grown up, things had been very different, and by and large remained so.

'The respect you had for the old folk was really strong!

And you still have to show respect in their company back home now', said one of our black members.

The group felt that it might be the economic base of our British industrial society that aggravated, if not caused, the categorising tendencies. Edna knew what it was to have teenage sons and could see that those youngsters who were in paid employment provided a readily exploitable market to commercial interests. A youth culture seemed to have grown up largely because they had spending power to be cashed in on.

It felt strange to have to recognise that groups had to establish a power base, usually economic, before they were properly respected. It was Joan who reminded us however that Jesus had contradicted all the usual preconceptions we have about status and respect by simply placing a child before his hearers as an example of those who would enter the Kingdom of God.[9] It was then, and still remains, a most unexpected image and yet we fail to see the scandal of it because of our familiarity with and our romanticising of the story. We could not find a reference in any other major religion or philosophy where such a contradiction is made so starkly by the simple expedient of questioning and reversing the oppressive myths of ageism. Again, Jesus had pointed us to those who seem to be the powerless and categorised ones; those who know what it is to wait, and he had pronounced that they had a special place in the action in God's Kingdom.

G. Waiting with a purpose

Emma, a Methodist of long standing and well acquainted with her Bible, had prepared a list of biblical stories which had come to her mind which had links with the waiting experience. Over the next few weeks of our meetings we were able to discuss many of them in detail. In the Hebrew Scriptures we first looked at the Psalms. Madeleine had been reading through a rather pessimistic interpretation of Psalm 130,[10] but still herself felt that it carried a strong note of hope. The Psalmist sings of his or her waiting experience:

I wait for Yahweh, my soul waits for him,
    I rely on his promise,
My soul relies on the Lord —
    more than a watchman on the coming of dawn.
Let Israel rely on Yahweh
    as much as the watchman on the dawn!
For it is with Yahweh that mercy is to be found,
    and a generous redemption;
It is he who redeems Israel
    from all their sins.[11]

Far from being a Psalm of pessimistic anxiety, we agreed with Madeleine that the hope of the Psalmist here in the promises of Yahweh and their fulfilment is beyond question, despite the horrendous predicament that the people were finding themselves in. And it seemed to us that this theme of trust in Yahweh's faithfulness to his promise, and the wisdom of having faith in his promise being fulfilled, was repeated time and again in so many of the readings that Emma had listed for us. What was the Exodus narrative if not a story of learning to wait faithfully upon Yahweh in the Sinai wilderness to provide the promised land? Through the voice of the prophets came the same call to remember the promises of the faithful Yahweh and the apocalyptic writers too seemed motivated by a frenzied determination to look for the signs of God's promised activity. Neither was there any despair in dear old Simeon, that New Testament prophet, who had devoted his whole life to faithfully waiting to set his eyes on the promised Messiah. And when this was accomplished, he gladly and happily announced — 'Great, now I can die happy!'[12] Yet what impressed us about this faithful waiting upon God's promises, of which we found so much in the Bible, was that it was not a wallowing in an empty flag-waving triumphalism but, on the contrary, it went out of its way to confront the realities of suffering and anguish. It was in fact out of these very experiences of suffering that the plea for the swift fulfilment of the promised things of God issued.

This experience of faithful waiting seemed also to have been shared by Jesus himself as he waited upon God in preparation for his own ministry. This is recorded for us in the gospel accounts of the temptation of Jesus in the wilderness.[13] We read the passages through very carefully a few times and John noticed an interesting parallel between our experience and this biblical passage. He had noted that the temptation stories are set between the baptism of Jesus in the Jordan and his forthcoming ministry. That was very reminiscent of the Old Testament sequence of the passing of the people of Israel through the waters of the Red Sea, later issuing in the taking of the Promised Land. In between these events had likewise come a period of fasting and temptation in the Sinai wilderness. John had noticed that our own time of waiting, our 'desert' experience, had come soon after our commissioning service and yet before our new ministry in the project had really got going.

'It's a bit of a come down, you know. You have a really good send-off, like that commissioning service, and then the reality hits you. I suppose Jesus felt that even more after the excitement of his baptism. It puts you back a bit, and it makes you do some very hard soul-searching, that's how I feel anyway. It must have been terribly hard for Jesus.'

It had certainly been a similar experience for the early believers, who had gloried in the triumph of the Resurrection only to find themselves having to face the realities of suffering and powerlessness, even knowing the destiny to which they had been called.

In his telling of the temptations story, Matthew symbolises and personifies the world's evil understandings of mission as the work of the Devil and the first temptation that Satan places before Jesus is to turn stones to bread and so to break his fast. We tried together to discover the nature of this inducement. Beryl was quick to notice that in fact Jesus did provide bread for the hungry when he fed the five thousand and so the temptation was not simply a temptation to supply material needs. The point surely of Jesus' reply that 'Human beings live not on bread alone'[14] was that there were underlying causes of hunger that had to be addressed too.

Margaret took Beryl's point further. 'It would be no good if Jesus just coped with the symptoms of the world's troubles; he had to go deeper. He had to think about every word that

comes from God – he had to go really deep and sort out
what the cause of all the problems was and attack that.'

This temptation opened itself to many interpretations but
something rang very true to our project experience in what
had been said.

The second temptation, according to Matthew's story, was
for Jesus to cast himself from the parapet of the Temple in
full view of the crowds, without being hurt. It was clearly a
temptation to exhibitionism – 'Does the Devil expect him to
do it twice-nightly?' came the tongue-in-cheek quip. There
would be no humility in such an egotistical display. And yet
again the group was aware of the paradox that Jesus actually
is reported to have amazed the crowds by his powers.(15)

'But even in a simple thing like playing soccer,' interjected
Ray, 'a player at Wembley should be cheered for scoring
three goals. It's spectacular, but if he's only doing it to boost
his self-image and not for the love of the game, then we
question his right to the cheers. Jesus did amaze the crowds,
but not just to boost his own ego or status.'

We were reminded that when Jesus raised the dead
Lazarus to life, the most spectacular thing imaginable, he
certainly did not go to visit the town merely in order to amaze
them with his powers. He goes and sees their sorrow and we
are told that Jesus wept. That is how vulnerable his humanity
and power is.

The third temptation is the offering to Jesus of total domination, but on the devil's terms. It would be so easy for Jesus
to be in a position of authority by merely going along with
the structures of the Jewish and Roman hierarchies and no
longer being 'difficult' or proving a threat to them. In this
way it would be possible to overpower from within. It would
require an awful lot of compromise on Jesus' part but might
be politically expedient in the long run. Such was the
temptation.

Marjorie interjected: 'You know, all these temptations are
relevant to the Advice Centre.' Sue took up the point: "It's
true; even on that last one alone. Just think how much easier
it would be to accept the bureaucratic response to the problems we've found in the community! The bureaucrats have
already said to us that it can't work our way. It would be so

easy for the Advice Centre to become official and threatening and bureaucratic, just like the system we're trying to fight. We mustn't do it the devil's way. We mustn't let it be heavy-handed – talking over the desk at people.'

Likewise, quite clearly, the other temptations were pertinent to our Community Advice Centre project. Just as Jesus had been tempted to prove himself *to* himself so our project could very well become for us a mark of our own usefulness – designed to prove that we were needed. We hoped we were useful, but we should not want to use others by making them dependent on us in order to prove how indispensible, good and important we were. Our intention was not to focus attention upon ourselves but rather to point to the Signs of the Kingdom generated by God in the acted parable of the project, so that those Kingdom Signs themselves might be the liberating and evangelising word to us all. The temptation stories taught us that it was Jesus and his works which were to be named and proclaimed and it was not for us to set ourselves up as anything but his willing and nameless disciples and servants.[16]

'My hope is,' said Edna, 'that because we are reflecting all the time like this that we'll be so conscious of these temptations that we'll be less likely to fall for them.'

The theologically reflective aspect of the project could, if used aright, keep us from falling into the trap of the first temptation – to think that by providing an information service we had thus struck at the heart of the issues we were confronting. On the contrary, there was more to these problems of oppression and domination than 'bread alone'.

H. Unemployment

The temptation stories had taught us that it is good sometimes to be made to wait and prepare oneself carefully but there was still the conviction coming out of our waiting experience that sometimes waiting could be a joyless and useless water-treading exercise. Also at the Advice Centre we were not being affirmed and there was such a sense of loneliness about us that it all felt rather similar to the experi-

ence our society calls 'unemployment'. Most of our group
had known the horrors of that experience in the past and
some were going through it even now. We could recite
instances where marriages had come under dreadful strain,
people had turned to alcohol or gambling to numb the
sensation of unemployment and youngsters turned to violent
crime on our streets to vent their anger at their rejection and
impotence. Here was an example of waiting which was a
wasting and degenerative experience. I suggested to the
group that it would be interesting to turn to the biblical
passage in which St John records an incident in which a man
who had been ill for thirty-eight years is cured by Jesus.[17]
Jesus notices him at the Sheep Pool in Jerusalem, a pool
surrounded by crowds of sick people, blind, lame and paralysed, all waiting to be the first into the waters which became
therapeutic whenever they bubbled up. Like the unemployed,
he waits in line with little or no chance of success. And as
he waits so his society attaches a stigma to him for being
sick, just as today the unemployed are so often blamed for
their plight. The unwaged have to wait about at the mercy
of the economic and political situation just as the paralysed
man relied upon the help of others if ever he was to get to
the pool. Even if he should be cured in the healing waters
it could only be at the expense of those who did not get there
first, just as the programmes run today to teach job applicants
to present themselves well to employers are only engaging in
a conspiracy of queue jumping. The vast majority still stand
and wait and the whole situation seems almost designed to
set the oppressed against one another as they have to fight
each other for the right to work.

Madeleine wondered about the obvious fact that many who
are unemployed do not really appear to want a job in any
case, preferring to wait around. Sometimes a 'sour grapes'
mentality could set in after many unsuccessful attempts to
get employment, and there would always be the few work-
shy who do not want to work at all. The man by the pool
likewise may not have been all that concerned about a cure
anymore after thirty-eight years, and Jesus even asks him
outright if he really wants to be cured or not. We could well
understand how this paralysed man had got to the stage of

being accepting of his situation for we knew from experience the fear which overtakes the unemployed at the thought of stepping out into a new place in society to find a type of employment so different from anything they've known before. Unemployment has become its own institution which can contain and control the human spirit and paralyse us in our fear of freedom and risk. The paralysed man is institutionalised and seems to prefer the society he has come to know rather than risk the cure and be plunged into all the turmoil of the wide world outside. How similar that all felt to today's state of institutionalised waiting in unemployment. The man gives his rather feeble excuse for not having been healed in all those years but Jesus does not seem to be interested in his answer and cures him anyway – he gives power to the unnoticed man waiting in the queue.[18]

Many of those attending at the Community Advice Centre were not in paid employment. Many had tried desperately but to no avail to find a job, some had given up, some had not bothered to try. The government work experience programmes for the unemployed had been some small attempt to turn waiting time into preparation for employment but when all the economic and political signs showed no likelihood of providing future jobs for so many, the question that these preparation programmes begged was 'preparation for what?'

It had been possible for us to adopt a quite positive approach to our own waiting at the Community Advice Centre and the bible study of the temptations had encouraged us to use our waiting time to take stock and prepare, but for many of those attending the Centre, things were not so encouraging. Their waiting was often waiting in such powerlessness that they had lost all hope and enthusiasm for the future. The man waiting for thirty-eight years by the pool was empowered by Jesus and his waiting was over. For some, like us, waiting could be experienced as a God-given opportunity for refreshment or preparation. But, for so many of our friends who visited us at the Community Advice Centre, their powerless waiting was truly a hellish experience and such an obscene waste of persons.

Our investigation into the 'waiting experience' had brought

us thus far but all the marginalised, the disabled, elderly, unemployed, black or young people, were all alike pointing us towards the much more vital issue of *powerlessness*. As we gained more experience over the first months of the project, so our work simply made us more aware of the inadequacy of our society to cope and care and our powerlessness to solve its problems. Where we had a success at the Community Advice Centre, we knew it to be at the expense of all the others who stood in line. Yet we had also found that these people in their powerlessness were helping us in some way to appreciate much more the dilemmas and joys of life, and were taking us into deeper awareness of this basic paradox of the power of powerlessness. What we had now learnt was that we needed to do some tough theological reflection upon this central and key issue for British society today, the issue of 'Power and Powerlessness'.

6: What Does 'Power and Powerlessness' Really Mean?

The question of 'Power and Powerlessness' was the basic question addressing us in our Community Advice Centre experience. The example of Jesus' incarnation spurred us to put ourselves with the powerless, just as Jesus had done – to put ourselves there not as patronising do-gooders with all the answers but as fellow servants. In this way, we were seeing at first hand the sorrows of powerlessness, experiencing more starkly our own powerlessness and yet paradoxically looking expectantly for Signs of the Kingdom of justice, power and love. Margaret reminded us that the cross which stood in our own church sanctuary was somewhat symbolic of this very paradox. It showed Christ imposed upon a wooden cross and yet the figure of Jesus was itself not held down by the cross behind it, but seemed to be rising above it. A picture of suffering it certainly was and yet, in all that powerlessness, the cross even there did not hold him captive. Could our Community Advice Centre parable in any way be pointing us to a clearer understanding of this mystery of the power of powerlessness and how it acts within and upon history?

A. Power takes many forms

Many of our meetings were spent telling stories about our own experiences of power and of powerlessness. We spoke of those who seemed to have power and of those who did not. We looked at individuals who had power, and groups or structures which manifested it. We examined carefully the experience of working alongside powerless people at the Community Advice Centre. We role-played examples, drew diagrams and pictures; we 'brain-stormed' ideas in order to be as expansive as possible; we worshipped, sang songs and battled through the disagreements until we were able to find our way through the maelstrom and classify different forms of power. Eventually, the group decided that a working distinction could be made between five forms of power but one person or institution could have a combination of these at its disposal at any time, for the forms interrelated in remarkably interdependent ways. Our classification worked out like this:

(i) Physical power

Most of us in our group could claim to have the physical power to control our muscular activity and yet in hospital we willingly relinquished our physical power into the hands of the surgeon or, on the streets it could easily be dominated by a violent gang of muggers. We felt that a working-class community like ours would probably be more aware of the important presence of physical power than some other strata of our society. We were surrounded by the visible evidence of it in the industrial architecture of our area and in the smoke billowing constantly from the nearby power station. We noted too that a respect for manual work and physical prowess had been important to the working-class for many generations and we made mention of the fact that a reluctance to express points of view or differences of opinion physically was not so evident in our community as it may be in other cultures. But in our locality we could see physical power helping as well as hurting others. Gardens were dug by youngsters for the elderly, shopping and house-decorating done for the disabled or housebound.

It was obvious too that even in a democracy it is in the last analysis physical force, or the threat of it, which stops disintegration into chaos. But history, both ancient and modern, is too full of examples of brutal coercion that it can no longer be held that all legitimised force is automatically ethically justifiable. The British Police Forces on the rioting streets of England and the troops patrolling the streets of Northern Ireland constantly raise up for us the question of what is or is not righteous use of legitimated violence. We found out too that over half of the annual budget of the so-called 'super powers' (USA and USSR) is now absorbed by the costs of military physical power and the proportion of the overall costs of research and development which is invested for military purposes is terrifying.[1] The more we searched our newspapers and recounted experiences, the more the group became aware of the importance in today's world and in British society of sheer physical power.

(ii) Political power

On one of our charts we drew a very large question mark after the words 'Our Votes' because we were perfectly aware that the grinding machinery of party politics and civil service means that our real political power is severely limited. There were times however when we as a church had exerted political pressure and run campaigns to have policy decisions changed at local and central government level. We spoke together of such things as our involvement in the 'Lead in Petrol Campaign' and of our work to change local road systems and the continuing work on the issues which our Community Advice Centre experience was leading us into. Here were examples of our own use of the pressure group techniques of political power.

Our attempts actually to define political power did not meet with much success. In the complexity of today's society, those who hold political power seemed often limited to the role of broker between many economic and military power groups rather than being strictly in possession of that power for themselves. Usually their only real power was that of influence and legislation. Political practice therefore called for a certain flair for diplomacy and ingratiation, but this was an art rarely mastered by those of high calibre.

One of our greatest difficulties perhaps was to understand the complex balance of political power which resides in the hands of those on the permanent civil service staff and that which must stay with the elected representatives of the populace at national and local levels. We laugh at the 'Yes, Prime Minister' television series because we sense that underlying the humour is a fearful truth about power in high places. But an even more mysterious enigma was presented by the apparatus and machinery of government itself, for although the official procedures, forms, protocols and practices have no life in themselves, they uncannily stamp what could almost be called their 'personality' upon those who serve them and upon those who supposedly are served by them. The power of the 'structures' of society seemed to be much more than simply the aggregate of their parts. 'Our experience at the Advice Centre sometimes makes me feel that the political system is in control and only rarely can a human person do anything to change it!' said Emily.

(iii) Economic power

Here was the power which it seemed could buy all the other forms of power. But as we chatted about it, so we realised that it really is more subtle than that, for when comparing economic power with military power it was difficult to decide which was the tail and which was the dog. On the one hand, the reason that white settlers and not the original Indian inhabitants own the oil in the USA is because the settlers beat the Indians into submission in warfare and then took the ownership of the land by force. The history of the British Empire tells the same story of physical power leading to economic power. On the other hand, however, it can be argued that it was in the last analysis economic superiority which enabled the military defeat of those poorer nations. We also recognised that the multi-national companies today have amassed such economic power that they can bypass the system of checks and balances on power crystalised in national and international law, whenever it seems in their interest.[2] One of our group evenings was spent pondering over copies of the *New Internationalist*[3] magazine which gave us ample evidence and lots of pictures and diagrams of how this happens.

The economic power in our own little group, laughable by comparison, was nevertheless real. We had limited choices about purchasing but we could choose to support certain brands or shops against others. Recently, our church began the selling of special tea and coffee imported from Sri Lanka on a fair-trade basis. This campaign certainly did not swing the balance of unjust world trade structures but what little economic power we had was thereby used more justly. We also agreed that those of us in paid employment had some small economic power by virtue of our union membership but we were reluctant as a group to put too much faith in our work unions, since they were equally as egoistic as the employers' federations. Yet power was undoubtedly there, where the unions had grown secure enough to inflict pressure and utilise their economic muscle.

(iv) Cultural power

A number of the group had read magazine articles which showed that over a period of time economic power accumulates in fewer and fewer hands, unless the process is deliberately checked, which is most rare.[4] Because of this accumulation of wealth, individuals or corporations are able to accrue to themselves the additional power of research and technological development which requires vast investment and puts them ahead of competitors. Their advertising, through their ownership of the communication media, gives a certain power over the minds and opinions of millions and this in turn acts as reinforcement of the present economic system, whatever that might be, and ensures a further entrenchment of power. This we noted was an example of economic power accruing to itself Cultural Power, which is the power to persuade others to accept a certain view of the world as normative. The education system, family structure, health services, architects, planners, musicians, and so many others are involved in creating an environment for us which dominates us so subtly that we hardly notice the extent to which we are swept along by it, like fish who hardly notice the water in which they exist simply because they are so conditioned to its constant presence. We are intimately affected by the larger environment but we also belong to sub-groups and sub-cultures within it and they exert subtle pressures upon us too by requiring a certain conformity of us if we are going to be accepted by them – and we readily conform because we human beings don't like to feel that we are excluded from any group.

It's interesting in this context to remember that in some respects the church itself is a sub-culture and it likewise

exerts powerful influences upon its members. Its cultural
power is exemplified in its use of powerful myths, inculcated
at an early age by Sunday School teaching and reinforced
through a continuing programme of education for adults.
Additionally, it utilises the constant repetition of cultic practice and edifying stories, and cements all this by means of
common action and work together. It is a cultural power
which the Church hopes to use for the good of all. The
Parables in Action group were concerned to remember
however that especially in olden times the church missionary
societies had attempted a similar programme of cultural
education abroad but had unwittingly been guilty of cultural
invasion and domination which could only be fully appreciated for what it was with the help of hindsight. Cultural
power then, even when in the hands of the Church, is like
other forms of power in that it can be used for either good
or ill.

As a church congregation set in a community, we were
trying to use our cultural power to demonstrate, by virtue of
our interracial make-up, the possibilities of breaking down
the barriers of prejudice. We were also proud of having built
up in our little church a strongly democratic culture and,
despite the inevitable tensions that sometimes ensued, we
nevertheless appreciated the cultural powers we thus shared
and which allowed us to cut and thrust in theological
discussion in our Parables group.

(v) Spiritual power

In no sense did we wish to give ourselves the impression that
God was inactive in the forms of power we had already
delineated, but there was a sense in which we felt that in
addition, spiritual power could be manifested in a particular
or specific manner. We could talk of the power of prayer, of
preaching, and of faith, but in trying to define our experiences, we centred in on two areas. Firstly, there was an inner
conviction which seemed to empower us as individuals but
which was difficult to define without recourse to perhaps
over-used words. Personal *faith* seemed to be the experience
we were talking of, and if we stripped from this word its
passive and sentimental overlays then we had some working

description of the experience. Christians, we could say, by virtue of their faith could be powerful individuals and we wanted to stress that this faith was more in itself than just an emotion or feeling – it was the welling up of an inner God-given urgency into an act of will and faithful action, for faith without committed action could hardly be called faith at all, or so our Advice Centre experience was teaching us.

Secondly, we felt that there was a kind of spiritual power which was evident and felt most when Christians were acting in fellowship together rather than simply individually.

' "When two or three are gathered together in my name" . . . there is a power to be reckoned with', exclaimed John.

This power was something like an energy of solidarity, fellowship and togetherness – or as the New Testament calls it, *koinonia*. Despite the many differences between us as Christian people, when we meet together across the denominations, we sense that there is a 'common coinage' of experience and commitment which is more than just a superficial agreement to belong together. There is a gift of solidarity, fellowship and trusting power, this power being felt as confidence together and a concern, as kindred spirits, for the Kingdom of God. At least, that's how we felt in our ecumenical project.

As we discussed our experiences, however, there was the inevitable tension around the group between those who wanted to stress the individual nature of the experience of spiritual power and those who wanted to say that the corporate *koinonia* experience was primary as an activity of God's Spirit. How difficult it was for us to realise that God's activity in the life of one member was not always immediately translatable into the experience of the rest. Added to this was what we felt to be a tendency in our British culture to prefer to think in individualistic categories – and amongst the working class specifically, there was a conservative notion that corporate activity was in some sense subversive, whereas personal feelings were more safe and socially acceptable to those in authority. This seemed to be something rather new to British working class culture who had always been romantically viewed as a communal people.[5]

We spent much time drawing diagrams and discussing personal faith and corporate fellowship, slowly beginning to acknowledge the presence and power of each, and as we did, so we began to realise that it was specifically this spiritual power of which we were wanting to know more, for it seemed in some strange way to be equally related to states of powerlessness as to states of power. The whole business of power was proving again to be ambiguous and tantalising. Having given careful attention to the different categories of power we set about looking at this ambiguity in more detail.

B. Power is not straightforward

In British society, it is taken for granted that there is high status in power, but it is also considered undignified ever to admit that one has it in abundance. Perhaps we are fearful that Acton's oft misquoted maxim may contain truth, that: 'Power tends to corrupt, and absolute power corrupts absolutely', and rarely does anyone complete the quotation which complains that 'Great men are almost always bad men'.[6] On the other hand, to admit to being powerless seems also to carry a stigma few are prepared to bear. This reluctance came to light particularly in the group when we were discussing death and dying. Did we not have an awesome fear of powerlessness and lack of achievement when we thought of our own demise? And yet the group refused to believe so. It seemed that most of the group did not feel that the future held any more insecurity than had the past, even though we acknowledged that death was a taboo subject in many quarters. There really seemed to be no front on which the group was prepared to admit its powerlessness and they steadfastly maintained that it was always possible to do something! Underlying these expressions of extraordinary faith in self-determination lay many factors. Firstly, it was quite clear that no-one in the group wanted to surrender themselves to fate and self-forgetfulness.[7] It was far too frightening to look the powerlessness of death in the face. Secondly, there was an understanding here of the self as a very active agent and perhaps without this strong self-image, one's standing in an

aggressive system would be impaired and one would soon go
under in the cut and thrust of working-class life. Additionally,
there seemed to be a kind of inverted fatalism amongst us
which made light of the precariousness of working-class life.
And we were meeting this fatalism not only in ourselves but
also in those we met at the Community Advice Centre.

We were brought down to earth at last when we thought
seriously about the experience we were having at the Advice
Centre. There we had to admit that although even the offer
of tea and sympathy could sometimes be of real value, nevertheless, when it came to achieving the changes required in
society to alleviate the intense suffering, in the end all that
we were very often doing was sharing in powerlessness.

'It makes you feel so angry that the ideals in the Bible are
not being achieved for people. Why should a person suffer
like that?' Colin looked pensive and then added, 'At first I
objected very strongly but the more I think about it, *powerlessness* is the right word for what we're experiencing. We are
powerless to achieve what we want to achieve, not only
personally but in trying to achieve for and with other people.
Standards of living for others, the ways people are treated
and the way society is run and structured – we are absolutely
powerless to get it the way we want it. You can help people
individually, but when it comes to changing the society for
the better, we're almost powerless to help'.

At the Community Advice Centre, it was sometimes possible to pull strings in the system which would help an individual with his or her own particular problem; but that same
structure within which we had pulled strings was responsible
for hurting countless millions of others for whom no strings
were pulled.

Madeleine hazarded a definition of power as 'the ability
to change the direction of something'. Now it was clear that
this power to change was seldom in our own hands. Sue
pondered, 'That's the agony of being human, You've got an
eye somehow or other fixed on perfection, on heaven, and
you've got some idea of what it should be like, but you just
don't have the power to do it – because of everything that
you lack. And even when we do seem to have the power we
use it badly, so that even when we know what we want to

achieve and have the power to achieve it, we can still end up working against our own better judgement'.[8]

C. Big but not beautiful – the power structures

Power in the hands of individuals was problem enough but in our work at our Community Advice Centre we were experiencing how bad things could get when power became faceless and when no individual could be held accountable.

'No-one seems to take responsibility any more', explained Margaret. 'They just hand you on from one department to the next. You can never get anyone to say "The buck stops here"; and no department official will ever give you their name'.

When power is in the hands of individuals, their responsibility is clear but when in the hands of groups, then something odd takes over. It happened that our discussion that evening was taking place in my own home and I remembered reading a passage by the theologian Niebuhr on this very theme. I quickly found the book and read the section to the group.

' . . . all these achievements are more difficult if not impossible, for human societies and social groups. In every human group there is less reason to guide and to check impulse, less capacity for self-transcendence, less ability to comprehend the needs of others and therefore more unrestrained egoism than the individuals, who compose the group, reveal in their personal relationships. The inferiority of the morality of groups to that of individuals is due in part to the difficulty of establishing a rational social force which is powerful enough to cope with the natural impulses by which society achieves its cohesion'.[9]

'You can see that perfectly well at the Centre', Alan continued. 'For example, suppose a visitor at the Centre is waiting for hospital treatment. Quite a lot of our elderly folk seem to be. Now you can be reasonably sure that doctors and nurses and hospital staff and administrators are all doing their very best to be caring and helpful, but the system itself doesn't allow the person to visit the hospital immediately and they sometimes have to wait for years in terrible pain. But you can't blame individuals for that'. It seemed that somehow our society as a whole had determined that those folk should suffer and that the priority for spending should not be hospitals but should be entertainment, nuclear armaments and the like. The group was realising that when the problem of evil power arose it focused quite sharply the distinction between individual responsibility and the reality of collective structures. Was there not more to hospital reform, for example, than simply converting all the staff to more moral attitudes and behaviour? There was the 'structure' which needed reform too, over and above the individuals within it. It took our group quite a time to sort out what terms we were going to use to describe what we were discovering and again we found the scholars helpful. The theologian Yoder came up with a helpful definition:

'The concept "structure" functions to point to the patterns or regularities that transcend or precede or condition the individual phenomena we can immediately perceive. The bridge is more than the cables and girders that compose it; the psychic 'complex' or 'syndrome' is much more than the thoughts and reflexes it organises; the 'class' is much more than the individual persons who make it up; a 'religion' is much more than a bagful of assorted practices. It is this patternedness that the word 'structure' tries to enable us to perceive within all the varieties of its appearance'.[10]

That single quotation made us realise just how all-pervasive the structures are and how much power they must hold in a complexly organised society such as our own. We even realised that week by week as our own small group met, so, depending on where we met and who attended, there would be a different group dynamic which was more than just the sum of the people there. So much depended on the structure of the group. Structures were so important that they were constantly being referred to in the Bible and it was to that source that we next turned.

Helped by a dictionary of the Bible and a Concordance, we found ourselves particularly fascinated by how St. Paul seemed to look at the whole subject. In one section, we found him being very positive indeed about the structures of society and Edna observed:

'I like what he says here, it makes good common sense. Because without any structures at all, our whole society would fall to bits, wouldn't it, so the structures around us help us to hold together'.

The way St. Paul had put it was to be found in the letter to the Colossians:

'In Him everything in heaven and on earth was created, not only things visible but also the invisible orders of thrones, sovereignties, authorities and powers: the whole universe has been created through Him and for Him. And He exists before everything, and all things are held together in Him'.[11]

We had to be guided by the Bible commentaries to find out that those final words – 'are held together' – translate a Greek word which comes from the same root as our word 'systematise'. The writer of the epistle was saying that the systems or structures are held together through and for Christ as honourable creations at his service. The New Testament agreed then with our commonsense view, that the 'structures' and 'powers' of a society are necessary to its functioning, and without them society as such cannot exist. In this sense they are a divine gift. Among them we felt we could list, for example, the religious structures, the 'ologies and 'isms, the moral structures of codes and customs, the political structures of nation, market or education. They are the systems of a society and are 'powers' in the land.

'The thing is,' said Ray, 'we've sorted out that these structures are very powerful and that they're good to have – given to us by God I suppose – but we've just said earlier that when evil and sin gets into them they can be even worse than really bad individuals. It's all very well Paul saying they're good to start with but we know they can end up pretty bad. It rather reminds me of the Book of Genesis where things begin perfectly in the Garden of Eden but then everything goes wrong'.

At this prompting we looked very carefully at the first eleven chapters of the Old Testament which seemed to provide a backdrop against which the rest of the Bible story was then played out. It explained that, although the original intent of God's creation was good, it was now infected by an evil whose nature was many-faceted, from the personal sins of Adam and Eve, the fratricidal injustice of Cain through to the Tower of Babel – that ultimate structure against God's authority. In Genesis we seemed to have an early analysis of the various aspects of sin and the consequent dislocation in the nature of the cosmos. When we then looked back to what St. Paul had to say we could see that although he was using the more cosmological language of his own day,[12] he was nevertheless saying something very similar. The Colossian epistle, for example, first says that all things are 'held together' or 'systematised' in Jesus, but later on explains that even these systems have been corrupted and can hold our hearts and attitudes in their evil power.[13] So in his epistle to the Romans, Paul describes the structures and powers as having fallen so far that they actually try to 'separate us from the love of God in Christ Jesus'.[14] But nevertheless, Paul was wanting to stress the fact that even given this fallen state the structures and powers can still serve some godly purpose. He is at pains for example to declare that even the Law, that powerful Old Testament structure which prevents us from full sonship, is nevertheless righteous and good at its heart and to be obeyed by those born under it.[15] Elsewhere he explains that in a similar way, the structures and ideologies which operated amongst the Gentiles had brought God's will to their attention initially, although these same ideologies were now holding the nations in bondage.[16] So Paul was telling his readers to be fully aware of the absolute power and final authority of God but also recognise that the power of these fallen structures, although temporary, is demonic and monstrous.

D. The nature of the Beast

Some readers have found it strange that Paul's epistles bear little witness to the teaching ministry of Jesus but dwell constantly upon testimony to the suffering cross of Christ as the element essential to the life of the new churches to whom he writes. This is largely because the early Christian groups were having to undergo dreadful persecution and suffering at the hands of the Roman Empire and so the shared experience of suffering love became the basis of solidarity between the young churches, Paul the apostle and their crucified Lord. They therefore had to confront the paradox of suffering horrendous persecution at the hands of the State and yet at the same time being aware of so many of its blessings. A theology which could cope with the ambiguity of the power of the Empire to guard against chaos and at the same time cruelly to oppress, had to be worked out in the pages of the New Testament and this endeavour largely colours the Scriptures as they have come down to us.

The New Testament traditions started to take on a glaring relevance for us now as we began to perceive that the ambiguities of the early Christians' predicament were so very akin to our own. We too had to live in and against the state, receiving all its many benefits and yet also aware of the insidious compromises it required of us. We too were in the world and yet not of it.[17] We were being forced by our Community Advice Centre experience to attempt an analysis of these forces in our society and as we searched the pages of the New Testament with renewed excitement so we discovered that St. John the Divine in his Book of Revelation had developed an analysis of similar factors of domination in the structures of the Roman Empire of his day. It was therefore to that book that we now turned in our Parables in Action group reflection. Over a period of many weeks we slowly managed to find our way through his maze of images, always wondering if his Revelation would be able to help us to understand the nature of what we were confronting today.

St. John is imprisoned, a captive in the Roman penal colony on Patmos Island, and writes a cryptic letter describing his imaginative vision. He tells of a battle in heaven and the dragon, the ancient serpent who is also called the Devil or Satan, is thrown down to the earth. So now heaven rejoices in the victory but the serpent turns in vengeance to wreak evil upon the earth by calling from the sea a beast which mirrors Satan's own attributes and with the appearance of the third beast from the earth, the unholy trinity is complete. The beasts have horns to represent their power and they are joined later by the figure of a harlot who represents the compromising ambiguities of the City of Rome.[18] The Beast's Empire then makes inhuman demands upon the people and in chapter thirteen a statue of the Beast is set up and all have to worship it. All the people chant adoringly, 'Who is like the Beast; who can fight against him?' (13:4). Then we read that 'He compelled everyone – small and great, rich and poor, slave and citizen – to be branded on the right hand or on the forehead and made it illegal for anyone to buy or sell anything unless he had been branded with the name of the Beast or with the number of its name'. (13:16–17) So without the mark of the Beast, the market place itself was closed to the people.

'Ah, that's so much like it is today', Marjorie sighed. 'If our shoes are from South Korea and our coffee is from Brazil, and our radio produced by some international company and our car is burning leaded petrol, then we're marked by the Beast's trade-mark aren't we! And there's no way out of it. They've got you haven't they!'

At every turn the Beast demanded compromise and subservience. Throughout the Roman Empire there grew the oppressive feeling of being taken over by an alien machine of taxes, customs and beliefs, and made to worship Caesars who claimed to be God. In the face of this machine, individuals were powerless unless they succumbed to its requirements, internalised its demands and made them their own. We began to feel as a group that our society today demands similar complicity and the person who would stand out against it will be stigmatised and accused of either being intolerant, a naive dreamer, or even a Marxist!

As our study of the Revelation image of the Beast came to an end, so we had become aware that even to function sanely in our present society without 'doing homage' and compromising constantly, is near to impossible. Everything seemed to be stacked against us. It was becoming evident that as the New Testament stated the matter, 'our fight is not against human foes, but against cosmic powers, against the authorities and potentates of this dark world, against the superhuman forces of evil in the heavens'.[19]

E. Living in a State

One evening, our Parables in Action group role-played a number of characters. The portraits used for the role plays were largely derived from case-histories presented in the introductory chapters of a book called *In and Against the State*[20] since the characters there, although very much in keeping with our community, were clearly anonymous and allowed for our role-playing to proceed more imaginatively. Each of us took a character, read through the description of their circumstances and, using our Advice Centre experience, tried to take on that person's role as if it were our own. The rest of the group then interviewed us in character. In this way, we got to feel what it was like to be that person.

Edna first role-played the part of Maureen, a mother of six, who had brought up her children on a Social Security income without the help of a husband. She had learnt to work the system and somehow or other to get by. Edna later confided that she had not found it difficult to get inside the role since she had great respect for the Maureens of this world. Maureen had gained much wisdom in handling the Social Services and other government structures but as we learnt from Edna afterwards, she felt powerless against the state and its machinery. She simply felt that she could not win but had learnt that 'if you're nice to the officials you might get what you're entitled to'. Edna had related how Maureen's mother had had a similar struggle long before the State had provided an official welfare apparatus, but Maureen had voiced her own belief that although the struggle had been financially harder for her mother, nevertheless the fear at the heart of her own anxiety was that being so dependent upon the State, it was always possible that the State would take the children away from her. That was a fear her mother had never had to cope with. The group asked her if she ever felt angry to be so dependent. Didn't she ever feel like getting together with others and campaigning about her situation? 'I've got enough worry with my own family without bothering about anyone else', she replied. She knew that in order to survive, she had to do everything the State's way.

'What choice has she got?' asked Edna. 'She had to submit

to the authority of the Beast and she felt the threat of it, but she had no alternative'.

Ray next role-played his part – a bus driver working for a nationalised company. Here was a nationalised service industry owned in theory at least by the community it was designed to serve. The driver had no romantic illusions though, and vividly described the ways in which the structures of management and union, of government funding and employee anger and frustration, had led to a situation where the standards of service had declined and the travelling public were no longer considered to be the first priority for the industry. Even this State service had in fact all the marks of conformity to the Beast upon it. Those employees who were intent on offering their very best to the public had to do so within the parameters set by the system, and those limitations were becoming more stringent and impersonal as time went on. 'I just have to make the best of a bad job', complained Ray, as he felt his way into the character of the driver.

It was as we were discussing the bus-driver's feelings that an important disagreement surfaced amongst the group. First of all, Colin observed that the driver could of course have been miserable at his work simply because of personal trouble at home and it may have had nothing to do with the structures of his job at all. This led some of the group to question again the relative importance of the individual as opposed to the pressures of society. Marjorie all along had been keen to stress the personal and individual aspects of the religious experience and she felt that this accorded very much with her own experience of the faith. Talk about society and structures in a religious context was rather foreign to her. Quite a healthy tension was focused in the group between those who felt their faith in personal terms and those who had experience of the work of the Spirit more within communities and groups. In a society which stresses its belief that all individuals are free, it was not a simple matter to concentrate on the powers that structures have in limiting the power of individuals. Louise asked Marjorie to recollect that as an individual moved up through the structures of power in an attempt to change society for the better, there was every likelihood that the structures would influence that individual to such an extent that he or she would no longer really want to change things so radically after all. The power of the structure would prevail over the individual. Colin too felt this tension between the importance of the individual and the importance of the structures when he called us to question whether it could ever be right for a Christian to set aside the first-aid task of caring for the symptomatic hurts of people in order to attend to the underlying social malaise which might be the cause of that suffering.[21]

'Can we possibly say – "Blow you for twenty years, die and suffer and struggle and we'll have a go at the root causes of your problem?" I know that's a bit too clear cut', observed Colin, 'but there's some truth in it'.

Whilst agreeing with Colin, we nevertheless had to own up to the fact that the Christian Church through the ages seemed to have been more concerned to ignore the root societal causes of suffering all together and had spent its energies only in alleviating individual symptoms. The myth had thereby been created, or at least reinforced, that the symptoms were all that really mattered to the Church – or worse still – that the symptoms were the only reality. It all reminded us so much of the temptation laid upon Jesus in the wilderness to ignore basic causes and issues and turn stones into bread, thereby alleviating immediately only the symptoms of need.

Our own group's reluctance to admit of the power of structures and ideologies was simply a reflection of the reluctance of the State to allow such questions to be asked or such structures to be perceived. The State's cultural power, as we had termed it, was used as a safeguard against such perception.

'But that's just like it is with a mental illness', said Colin. 'One of the reasons a mental illness keeps its grip on a patient is because the patient can't see it, just can't see it. The doctor or psychiatrist's job is to help the patient see the actual cause of the problem, then there's a chance they'll get better but usually the real cause has been deeply hidden in the unconscious and not allowed into the open'.

We slowly began to feel that just as the psychoanalyst seeks to interpret to the patient the machinations of their inner myths and turmoils, so too the social scientist could try to bring us to an awareness of the machinations of the under-lying forces of society. In that way we might become more conscious of causes and not just of society's symptoms and so become more open to the possibility of real healing.[22] But we were only too aware that such critical awareness would never be won easily. If we were anything to go by, then we would have to recognise that in our British society there is a tremendous reluctance to think this way. So it was that Sue told us of an article that she had read in preparation for the meeting which related the experience of those govern-ment sponsored advice centres up and down the country which had decided to turn from first-aid work with individ-uals, to group work with those who were suffering from local housing deprivation. They immediately came under fierce attack from city councils who claimed that they would have to review the operation of such advice centres. It was clear that what was feared was the advice centres' growing aware-ness that society itself was often the cause of the ills of its poorest members, and not always vice versa, as the common wisdom would have us believe.[23]

John brought our attention to a similar situation when he referred to the work of the Community Health Councils, ostensibly a democratising element in the State's health care provision. Workers in these Councils however, when indi-cating that many of the causes of the illnesses with which they were confronted would seem to be the symptoms of societal and environmental factors, were told by the Area Health Authorities that funded them that such statements and observations were not part of their remit.[24]

'But that's what's happening to us now', said John. 'We've looked at the problems besetting our area and we've begun to realise that the cause of many of these problems is not actually in this community. But whenever you talk about the sorts of problems we're facing every day, people who don't live here say "Oh, that's your area, ours is OK!" What they don't see is how their area is all tied up with ours. That their "nice" place is all part of the structure that makes our area a "nasty" place, But how do you ever explain that to anyone?'

At this point, Sue became quite animated. 'What annoys

me', she said, 'is the fact that normally it's only the intelligensia and the middle-class trendies who get to know these things. The people that are really at risk, who really are hurt by all this, are never given the information. It's only because we're learning to understand theology in the Parables in Action group that things are becoming clearer for us – and goodness knows it's taken us a lot of hard work to unearth it. It's like a big unconscious conspiracy on the part of all of us in society!'

'Ah, now we're getting back to the Beast again!' said Marjorie.

F. Can good win?

The image of the Beast or monster had recurred again and again in literature and art alike. We flicked through art books and admired the lurking monsters in the paintings. Madeleine had enjoyed reading Mary Shelley's great nineteenth century classic *Frankenstein* and gave us her interpretation of it.

We had all seen the movies of course, and to begin with many were amazed to learn that Frankenstein was not the name of the monster at all but of its creator. Dr. Frankenstein had combined medieval alchemy with modern chemistry and discovered the secret of imparting life, Madeleine told us, but as soon as the creature breathed, Frankenstein assuming he had made a diabolical mistake, ran away, leaving the creature to find its own way in the world. But strangely the creature turned out to be naïve and benign and it was only as it was met by society that it turned to evil and murderous corruption. Madeleine read the passage where the monster itself pleads, 'I was benevolent and good, misery made me a fiend. Make me happy, and I shall again be virtuous'.[25] But by now Frankenstein feels powerless in the face of his own creation and at the last can only set out to destroy it or let it destroy him. The story of Frankenstein so clearly portrayed the fact that evil seems to have the power to take what is created good and turn it to monstrously evil purpose. It could do this to individuals just as it could do it to the structures of society. The body politic, created as St. Paul held, to defend society from the chaos of barbarity, now could even threaten to separate us from God's Love.[26] We thought too of our European experiences of how the evils of Hitler's Third Reich had infected the whole German nation and how that hatred had spread to our own nation once we too had been gripped by warfare.[27] We reflected upon how the wonderful discovery of nuclear power had sunk us into the present miseries of the stock piling of nuclear armaments. It seemed that things could not really get much worse.

At a more local level, we had experienced at our Community Advice Centre project the damage which could be visited upon the weak of our society by its inhuman power to control the lives of its members. And so many decisions which deeply affected the lives of our people seemed to be made without their consent by a faceless bureaucratic 'them'.

As we contemplated these negative aspects of our experience, Madeleine brought us to the crux of our questioning and concern:

'I find it extremely difficult to believe that we can overcome evil, it seems to me that evil is getting stronger and stronger. I cannot see good winning. If you try to take power yourself in order to beat evil, it seems so to infect you that you don't end up beating evil but become a part of it yourself. It's like a cancer'.

We wrote in large letters across our wall-board CAN GOOD WIN? Was there something in the powerful powerlessness of Christ which, without sentimentality or escapism, we could claim had proved strong enough to confront this basic question of faith, can good win?

7: The Power of Powerlessness

A. Help from the Early Church experience

Madeleine had voiced for us the central problem which demanded an answer. Our experience seemed so shot through at every level with evil that it really was difficult to see an end to it. And yet Christians believed in a God of Love who surely did not condone the suffering which was everywhere so evident. Had not God been responsible for every aspect of His creation then? Had He long since left the creation to its own devices or were Christians simply mistaken about ascribing generous loving qualities to the creator? Why did a powerful God seem to leave His creatures so powerless and what was He going to do about it? We were determined to confront this problem but so far we felt we had relied perhaps overmuch upon stories and symbols. Given the tough reality of the problem was there not a place here for some hard-headed logic? We had been fascinated and captivated by St. Paul's imagery of the 'principalities and powers' and by St. John's visionary story of the Beast but we had to remember that stories do have their limitations because they largely depend for their power upon emotional responses and the transplanting of the insights from the imaginary context of the story into the new and real context of the hearer where the insight is to be applied. This means that the story is open to being badly used, leading to an evasion of the realities and complexities of the new situation of the hearers.[1]

We therefore have to bring all the rational tools of the careful, critical mind to bear upon any insight learnt from stories just as we would to any other important discovery.

We were to find that there was no simple way out of the problem of evil for Christian thinkers. One slick answer had been to ascribe all evil not to God but to the Devil or Satan. This argument did not hold water however, for quite apart from the fact that not many of our number believed that the Devil existed in that sense, if he *had* existed then he would still have originally been created by the Almighty, so in the final analysis the responsibility still remained with God. There had to be a more convincing answer to the question of evil and to help us in our search we could call upon the early Christian thinkers and philosophers to assist us.

To begin with, most members of our group seemed to me to be favouring, quite unknowingly of course, an approach which St. Augustine had originally worked out, whereby all evil is attributed either directly or indirectly to the wrong decisions of free human beings. Some of the Anglicans had heard about St. Augustine before, so we looked up what he had to say about our problem in what is perhaps his most popular book, *Confessions*, which he wrote at about the time when the old Roman Empire was crumbling. We found a sentence which read: 'Free will is the cause of our doing evil and Thy just judgement is the cause of our having to suffer from its consequences'.[2] Augustine was arguing that God was not responsible for the evil and suffering in the world – He was too holy for that – but what evil did exist could all be attributed to human beings, using our free will selfishly and unlovingly.

We could see that if we followed Augustine's lead we would do justice to our feeling that God could not be blamed for the terrible things our Advice Centre work had brought to light. According to his theory, God clearly remained the Holy One and innocent of evil. But one problem remained. If God was going to allow us justly to suffer the consequences of our wrong-doing, on what basis of justice then did He arbitrarily select those whom He was going to save from these consequences? Could the God who reveals Himself so generously as divine and sensitive Love in the person of Jesus, at the same time distance Himself so from His creation as to arbitrarily select those whom He would save and those whom He would damn?

'You can't reduce salvation to a glorified Bingo game like that!' I objected.

The difficulty for those of us who could not go all the way with St. Augustine was that the alternative theory, originally propounded by Irenaeus, another early church writer, only served to leave us on the other horn of the dilemma. Irenaeus spoke of the world as an environment created by the truly loving God who had appointed every last detail of it in order to help humankind to develop within it from the immaturity of the fallen state up to the perfection that God wills for us.[3] The way he put it was to say that we are created in the 'image' of God, but that we will be brought, by the work of the Holy Spirit, to be the very 'likeness' of God, through experience of suffering and sorrow.[4] The world according to this view, is like the 'vale of soul-making' described by the famous poet John Keats in one of his letters.[5]

'The problem with that is that John Keats and Irenaeus didn't live through the last war', said Ray. 'I'm sure they're right to say we do learn from suffering, it helps us to mature and become much better people, but God's got a funny way of teaching us if He needs to have millions gassed and tortured to do it!'

Perhaps it was because the members of our group had come so close to the realities of suffering in our community that no-one was prepared to argue for the 'vale of soul-making' approach to the problem. It simply failed to do justice to the extent and horror of suffering in the world and even made evil out to be the servant and agent of the loving creator. But where Irenaeus had helped us was to bring to our attention the fact that we needed to find a way of seeing evil and suffering as somehow within the loving economy of God, since it was clearly there within His creation. Yet at the same time we had to witness, as St. Augustine had done, to the reality and full horror of domination and suffering in the world.

'Perhaps one way around this problem, "Can Good Win?",' thought Colin aloud, 'is to stop for a moment concentrating so much on evil and look to see where we can see good around us in the world. Then we can have a go to see if it can ever win, even with all this suffering around'.

This we decided to do but our earlier experience of looking for what we had called God's Unexpected made us feel that it could just be that we would find most good focused right there in those who on the contrary were exposed to the extremes of evil and suffering. Had not St. Paul taught us to expect this very thing when he spoke of his 'thorn in the flesh' and when he wrote so dramatically that,

'power comes to its full strength in weakness. I shall therefore prefer to find my joy and pride in the very things that are my weakness; and then the power of Christ will come and rest upon me. Hence I am well content, for Christ's sake, with weakness, contempt, persecution, hardship, and frustration; for when I am weak, then I am strong'.[6]

Colin gave us another example of the paradoxical strength and powerlessness of goodness by drawing our attention to a girl in Walsall who was completely paralysed and only by blowing into a special machine was she able to communicate – and yet what she communicated had such warmth and goodness about it. It derived from such powerlessness and yet it was charged with vitality and power. Likewise the majority of the New Testament seemed to be written by so-called powerless people who knew the realities of suffering and the smell of the inside of a prison. Even Jesus himself who had the power to set people free from captivity and oppression, and in whom were all the qualities of goodness, came in this same powerless way. Born in poverty, living in a vulnerable culture, speaking a minority language, dying a death designed for criminals, Jesus of Nazareth was looked to as Saviour and Liberator of those who followed him. 'And he expected them to follow him in the same way, taking up their crosses and suffering where necessary', continued Norah, 'and my goodness didn't they suffer!'

The suffering experience of the Early Church had demanded of them that they develop a workable theology for their predicament just as we now had to. They found their task was helped by the fact that many of the oral traditions which spoke of the suffering of Jesus offered keys to understanding and action in the face of domination and suffering and it was to this resource that we turned next.

B. The trials of Jesus

The sections of the Gospel upon which everything seemed to turn for us were those final episodes in Jesus' ministry when, after having been arrested, he is brought face to face with the powerful structures of evil and confronts them on their own territory. We each took a character and read through as dramatically as we could, the Lucan account of the appearance of Jesus before the Sanhedrin.[7] This experience helped us get behind the written page and into the feeling of the oral tradition which lay behind it. We thought for a moment together. The passage showed Jesus addressing his accusers with all their pomp and obsequiousness and yet not once did he grasp at status and prestige for himself but prefered to answer in terms of the authoritative servanthood of the Son of Man.

'What we've got here', said Edna, 'is not a passive Jesus at all. He really speaks out, but in a powerfully loving way. It's more of a bold humility, isn't it? To stand up there in that awe-inspiring atmosphere of the religious court and lay it on the line – that's very powerful indeed; but it's not self-acclamation. It's bold humility'.

A similar understanding was gained from our dramatic reading of Luke's account of Jesus' trial before Pilate and Herod.[8] Pilate's prime concern as a Roman politician was with the stabilisation of power and this accounts for his decision to please Herod by passing the prisoner also to him, since Herod happened to be in Jerusalem at the time. The passage makes it quite clear therefore, that Jesus is caught in the middle of a game of power politics, but even though he is brought before the emblazoned power of Rome itself and tossed back and forth between Herod and Pilate, Jesus still refuses to grovel. We know that Pilate had no great love for Jews,[9] yet Luke gives the impression that before Jesus even Pilate is weakened in his resolve to deal harshly. In Pilate's presence Jesus refuses to answer any charge directly and in this way refuses to invest any final authority in the Roman law and administration. In the few minutes that are allowed to him he says everything that need be said. According to him whatever happened in this Roman court was not in the final analysis authoritative; whatever titles they ascribed to Jesus and however harshly they dealt with him, his abiding concern was to remain the Kingdom and its advent. In this was his power.

So even in these trial scenes we could see a powerful Jesus; it was the same Jesus who, in his earlier ministry, had had power to forgive sins,[10] to do miracles,[11] and who was even acknowledged by the evil powers themselves.[12] At his trial Jesus was not merely accepting powerlessness, but rather he was choosing to take upon himself all the limitations which the Powers could impose upon him. It was the inevitable outcome of his incarnation, when God chose to be expressed within the full limitations of the human predicament.

'That's the agony of being human', said Sue. 'You see glimpses of the eternal, yet you're bound to your limitations – you're mortal – and you see all that agony in Jesus'.

St. Paul, in his letter to the Philippians, quotes a poem which speaks of this tension as being the essence of Jesus' story.[13] We read it together from the service of Evening Prayer.

'Christ Jesus was in the form of God: but he did not cling to equality with God. He emptied himself, taking the form of a servant: and was born in the likeness of men.

Being found in human form he humbled himself: and became obedient unto death, even death on a cross'.

Here was God's power made manifest in the ungrasping Servant Jesus, experiencing all our limitations and powerlessness without compromise.

Jesus manifests in himself the tension between eternity and mortality, divinity and humanity, power and powerlessness. He never simply collapses one into the other, but fully expresses both realities as he stands before the seat of Pilate but with his eyes fixed on the throne of God. It is a confrontational attitude which is only allowable and only has such overwhelming integrity in a human being who knows the self-limitation of love and powerlessness.

Edna said 'Is it that powerlessness is very acceptable to God?'

'No', said Colin perceptively. 'Isn't it rather that our servanthood is very acceptable to his Power?'

C. The Crucifixion

As we turned next to the gospel account of the crucifixion, we began to sense that it was here that Power and Powerlessness finally meet.

Vincent Taylor, in his commentary on Mark's Gospel, refers to crucifixion as one of the most abominable forms of torture ever invented. 'Naked and unable to move, the victim was exposed to pain and insult, enduring thirst and finally, sometimes after days, dying from exhaustion, unless mercifully his sufferings were brought to an end by a spear thrust or a shattering blow'.[14]

As we read the account in St. Matthew's Gospel,[15] we considered the ways in which the various forms of power, which we had distinguished, were now pitted against Jesus as he hung on the cross. Clearly the power of Physical Force held him bound to the tree at the will of the military guard. Political Power had engineered the death and had legitimised it in the world's eyes. Those who held Economic Power, who had so much to lose by allowing Jesus to continue his preaching against the abuses of the Temple and the evil pursuit of Mammon, had been at work, especially through the Sadducees and Herodians, to silence Jesus. He had crossed the holders of Cultural Power too when he had questioned the centrality of the Sabbath and the Temple, those symbols of nationalistic piety. Our fifth category of power – Spiritual Power – was in his own hands, but offered him the most enticing of all temptations, the temptation to use it to his own ends and grasp at status, dominion and show. All the powers of evil, individual and structural, had worked together to take him to the cross. It was vile and horrific: and we pondered upon the implications.

We wondered what St. Matthew meant by adding to the picture by telling of supernatural happenings which surrounded and followed the death of Jesus.[16] We read that a darkness shrouded the earth, the Temple veil was torn through, the earth quaked, and tombs gave up the resurrected saints. Such happenings put this death into a different category from that of the death of any other king or any other Lazarus. St. Matthew was impressing on his readers that even the cosmos shared the pangs of the event. Just as he stood before Pilate and Herod and denied their claim on him so now on the cross Jesus placed himself before all the powers of evil and refused to acknowledge their authority. For him, only God had the final and absolute authority. The whole group felt certain that he did not just accept the role but it was something he achieved. He got in amongst evil in all its horror and power, experienced its fullness, placarded it and advertised it, held it up for public display and confronted the authorities with their own evil and shame.

Jesus' death on the cross is no pathetic submission to or acceptance of death's authority either but a sinewy test of love. The cross demonstrates, firstly, his total solidarity with those who are oppressed by evil; secondly, it placards and displays evil's ugliness back to the world. Thirdly, through the cross Jesus makes God's ultimate protest against evil; and finally and profoundly, it brings the key to unlock history. These four elements could only be achieved by the powerful powerlessness of the cross. It seems folly to the wordly wise until they are asked how to defeat evil in any other way than by displaying the integrity of love.

When we read the words of John Yoder, an American scholar, we felt he had found the words for what we now wanted to express. He wrote of Jesus:

'His very obedience unto death is in itself not only the sign but also the first fruits of an authentic restored humanity. Here we have for the first time to do with a man who is not the slave of any power, of any law or custom, community or institution, value or theory. Not even to save his own life will he let himself be made a slave of these powers. This authentic humanity included his free acceptance of death at their hands. Thus it is his death that provides his victory: "Wherefore God has exalted him highly, and given him the name which is above every name ... that every tongue might confess that Jesus Christ is Lord." '(17)

D. Power without domination

'When we're working at the Community Advice Centre', said Alan, 'we're constantly overwhelmed by trying to be of use to people who really are in powerless situations. I can see that Jesus confronts these problems on the cross, but what does that tell me I need to *do?* What has the cross done, what difference has it made now to the powers and structures, the Powers and Principalities as St. Paul calls them, and how will that help now? I want to know if there is any way of approaching that question'.

It was my conviction that St. Paul in his letter to the Colossian church actually seeks to answer the question which Alan had voiced, and so the group agreed to spend time during its next series of meetings in studying that epistle.(18) The key section seemed to us to be in the second chapter where the writer pictorially describes what happened to the structures and powers at the crucifixion. The way he puts it is to say that Jesus 'discarded the cosmic powers and authorities like a garment; he made a public spectacle of them and led them as captives in his triumphal procession'.(19) We brought to the passage all that we had learnt from the project thus far in order that we might fathom the meaning underlying the now rather archaic language. We knew that Jesus had gone right to the political and spiritual heart of the nation and had confronted the powers of evil in their own stronghold. He had thrown the spotlight onto them and, as the passage says, had made a public spectacle of them, disrobing them and showing them to have no authority in their own right. He stripped them of their pomp and on the cross showed evil up for what it is. From now on, for those who had eyes to see, it would no longer be possible for the structures to masquerade as if they were basic or ultimate realities. The truth of the matter was now very different for those who were conscious of it. No longer could the structures dominate for they were now put back into their proper place behind Jesus 'in his triumphal procession'. He restored them to their rightful place in the order of things so that they may now be used to serve but without domination.[20] It is a reconstituting of the good creation itself that is going on here.

In the original creation and even in the constitution of our human nature, God had shown no inclination to dominate us and had even created us to some extent independent of Himself, so that we might have the opportunity to be free and self-determining. He had given us free will and did not counter that by dominating the freedom He had gifted to us. To some degree, He still takes a back seat in human experience and does not thrust Himself at us, although we are free to discern His loving and yearning presence everywhere. The creator had even been reluctant to force His hand upon the natural laws which He Himself had set in motion even though the dynamic inherent in them was problematic. If He ever did intervene it was purely to signify His loving kindness and generosity rather than to impose a nonsense upon the inevitable struggles which were the evolutionary implication of His creative genius. We had been given the structures, and we had even been given the faculty to create powers and structures ourselves so that within this independence we could use them to relate to the natural environment, and indeed they were indispensible to that end. Without structures we would live in ungodly chaos. Our recent learning had taught us to discern that a perversion occurs when, instead of these structures remaining necessary tools in the struggle, they are allowed to take on a dominating life of their own. That was what the pictures of the Fall and the Beast were all about. When Jesus confronts evil on the cross, in so doing he has restored creation at its heart and the structures are put back into perspective so that we can now demand that they are placed in a subservient relationship to humanity. If ever we see them attempting to usurp the place of God or humanity we are now at liberty to engage them and renounce them fearlessly. Only when they are fulfilling their proper serving function are they a blessing from God.

So we now understood that creation, including the necessary structures and powers, be they intellectual, moral, religious or political, is in every respect wisely constituted so as to allow us justice and love. In all this, God's constitution of the world was and is good. Within this framework Jesus has now also given us a proper appreciation of God's nature as He who will not dominate.[21] Our group project had taught us time and again that the underlying evil in human experience derives from precisely this yearning in individuals and in the structures to dominate and use power to their own end. This was the very essence of blasphemy. And it was against this tendency that Jesus strove and won. He displayed the power of resolute daring and service rather than domination, and thereby inserted the constant operation of God's Unexpected back into history. And the authoritative seal of the resurrection was set by God upon his servanthood thus ratifying this whole new state of affairs – it was the inauguration of the Kingdom of God.

8: Living The Alternative

A. Daring to say 'Jesus is Lord!'

'What we have to do is check all the structures and authorities that are around today to see if they fit into the pattern Jesus wants then', explained Ray. 'If they don't clearly follow behind him in his triumphal procession, as it says, then we don't give them the authority they demand'.

For us Jesus was now to be the measure of all things. The Early Church too we discovered, soon proclaimed its absolute belief that only Jesus was Lord and that the Powers no longer had final authority, for as they said, God had 'enthroned him at his right hand in the heavenly realms, far above all government and authority, all power and dominion, and any title of sovereignty that can be named, not only in this age but in the age to come'.[1] We were now wanting to proclaim his majesty but this realisation had only come to us as we had become more fully aware of the extent of Jesus' triumph, and this had only happened after we had faced up to the horrific social situations in our locality and beyond. We had looked fully at his suffering and death in the tragic circumstances of those around us and strangely we had thereby come to a stage where we were sensing more dramatically than ever the power of his resurrection. Our experience was in this way akin to how it must have been for the suffering early Christians, for when they made bold to proclaim that 'Jesus is Lord' they too were flying in the face of the harsh realities of suffering. They were in fact then making a very extreme political claim. Ronald Sider put this very forcibly when he wrote, 'to announce Christ's Lordship to the principalities and powers is to tell governments that they are not sovereign. It is to tell them that whether or not they know or acknowledge it, they are subject to the risen Lord Jesus who summons them to do justice, to seek peace, to promote *shalom* on the earth. It is to tell governments that Jesus Christ, who is one with the Father, is on the side of the poor and that He is at work in history pulling down the rich because of their oppression and neglect of the poor and exalting the lowly. Again it is clear that merely to witness in a biblical way to the principalities and powers is to engage in dangerous, subversive political activity'.[2]

This reminded us forcibly of Martin Luther King's sermon when he proclaimed 'I have a dream'.[3] True it was only a dream and yet he had a conviction about its authority that drove him on against all the odds. He knew that at the cross the victory was already won and the Powers put back in their rightful place. We had likewise heard that Nelson Mandela, the imprisoned South African leader, is known by his prison colleagues as 'The Smile' because despite the harsh reality of having spent most of his life locked up in prison for his beliefs, he knows that although he cannot see it now, he fights for a cause that is in the heart of God and that there is therefore an inevitability about victory.

It was that same final victory which was affirmed in the early credal statement that 'Jesus is Lord'. But in making this proclamation the early Christians were not necessarily seeking to be antagonistic to every form of government. They were not simply anarchists. But Paul's stern words in his epistle which exhorted readers to obey the State,[4] like John the Baptist's mandate upon his hearers to obey the authorities, would now have to be read and understood as being spoken from the context of the Bible's rigorous critique of governments and structures when seen from the perspective of the Kingdom of God. As St. Paul says, 'When anyone is in Christ, there is a new world order; the old order has gone, and a new order has already begun'.[5] The Christian who claims 'Jesus is Lord' is participating in God's power to change history, by serving as the Master served and using the powers as subservient tools to that end. Thus it was that although St. Paul had to acknowledge that the early Christians were being 'treated as the scum of the earth, the dregs of humanity, to this very day',[6] he could still be convinced that they were also the inheritors of the Kingdom and thereby already participants in the New Age.

And yet they were still not at liberty to make this a cause for selfish boasting or for falling back into a dominating piety or unrealistic triumphalism. There had been, from the first, the temptation to slip away from the servant role as we could see from the firm warning against this in the writings of St. John the Evangelist. He specifically omits from his gospel record of the happenings in the Upper Room the vital element of the institution of the Lord's Supper and substitutes instead the episode of the foot-washing. This must indicate to us John's fear that already in his time the practices of the contemporary church were raising eucharistic presidents to higher status than the servant image of the suffering Christ could possibly warrant. Instead, John's gospel account urges its readers to see in the seeming powerlessness of the crucifixion itself the true 'exaltation' and 'glorification' of the Son.[7] So it is that at the very moment when Jesus dies on the cross, John draws our attention to his cry of victory, 'It is accomplished!'[8] St. John knows that the temptation to slip away from the servant role and to use our power and influence to dominate is even there in the Church and its structures so he brings us up sharply and makes us remember that it is *as servant* that 'Jesus is Lord'.

To proclaim Jesus thus was also to deny that authoritative title to any other. Thus it was in the same confrontational spirit of service to the Kingdom of God that the early martyrs acknowledged the one supreme authority of the Lord Jesus, even as they stood condemned by the Roman authorities for refusing that title to the emperor. So often they are portrayed as passive pietists whereas any reading of their history indicates that they, in true pursuit of their master's way, were political subversives. Speratus, the spokesman of the Scillium martyrs is recorded as having said, 'I do not recognise the empire of this world; but rather I serve that God whom no man has seen nor can see'.[9] We were amazed to hear that

Dasius, the soldier, even went so far as to say, 'Do what you want, I am a Christian. I spit on and abominate your emperors and their glory . . .'[10] Yet even in this atmosphere the Early Church surprisingly did not attempt to overthrow the empire, but nevertheless made it perfectly clear that they would never allow it the authority to gainsay the ultimate power of the Almighty, the Lord Jesus.

By the same token, our discussion of the Beast figure in St. John's Revelation had made us appreciate that the Roman empire's claim to be ultimate, as symbolised in the cult of the emperors, was precisely that enemy with which Jesus, the 'Lamb', was engaged. The magnitude of the battle which ensues in the book of Revelation against Rome's blasphemy, shows us the hatred which John had for the imperial bombast. In his apocalyptic vision he saw that in the final analysis God's enemies are annihilated, but in the meantime our interim role is to engage in what the Quakers referred to as 'the War of the Lamb'.[11] By that they meant that Christians should participate in God's struggle with the rebellious world – to proclaim Jesus as Lord of Lords and remain obedient to his commands and strategies over against the claims and self-aggrandisement of the powers.

'The Quaker idea of the War of the Lamb seems to make sense as far as our Advice Centre is concerned', observed Marjorie, 'because we are trying there to do our part in the Kingdom – rather like "Thy will be done on earth" '.

'But we can see now that only if it's serving and caring will our powerlessness have any real power. It's not just a throw-away powerlessness that Jesus seems to be asking for. I find that very difficult', acknowledged John.

We felt that Jesus was relying on us to put ourselves into a situation along with the powerless, but not to knuckle under to the authority of what makes them powerless. To know we were engaging in the War of the Lamb would give us the faith and inspiration to go on even when everything seemed ranged against us and when we felt so very useless.

Caesar had set his mark, his number, upon those he claimed, just as the powers which dominate our society seek to make total claim upon our lives. We had come to realise that our consumerist culture grips our society in its technological and bureaucratic teeth with little respect for persons. It swallows our annual national budgets, our national education programmes, our health services, and all must owe some sort of allegiance if they are to survive at all. But if society wishes to brand us with the mark of the Beast, it has to reckon with the fact that the Lamb has already marked us for his own by the sign of Baptism so that we no longer belong to the old order but to Him.[12] Thus Matthew ends his Gospel with Jesus' words to his disciples, 'Full authority in heaven and on earth has been committed to me. Go therefore and make all nations my disciples; baptise them in the name of the Father and the Son and the Holy Spirit . . . and be assured I am with you always . . .'[13] It is this baptismal mark of Jesus' authority over us, the Sign of his abiding presence and power, which now overrides any allegiance that may be claimed of us by the Beast. No longer are our relationships clouded and perverted by the structures since when two or three are meeting together in the 'Name' then he is amongst us as Lord. This he has promised, and as one theologian has put it, 'the person with the promise is in fact the revolutionary'.[14]

B. Tools in the struggle

The mark of baptism binds us not only to Jesus but to one another in a fellowship which should stand over against Empire, using powers and structures in accordance with his serving anti-dominating will. There is room in God's Kingdom for structures and form but now they must toe the line and fall in behind Christ in his triumphant procession. Thus Christians are expected to work within the 'structure' of the Church, the fellowship of the Lamb, the Christian alternative community, for the full working-out of God's purposes. This is possible through the New Dispensation in history which allows for God's dynamic mix of power and servanthood to function, through God's grace, with our responsible participation. And it's all immensely exciting and challenging!

It was as we worked our way through to this conclusion

that we began to appreciate that in the process of this struggle the Church has been given the resources which can sustain us and be utilised by us in the War of the Lamb. During our project we had become particularly aware of the three great treasures which were to function as tools in the struggle.

(i) The Eucharist

One of the central features of the fellowship of Christian disciples has always been the eucharistic feast, that sacrament of the sharing community. Sitting at table with Jesus, intimately sharing his fellowship, his guidance and his presence had been a central feature of the ministry of Jesus to his friends. It had celebrated present joy and anticipated the future fulfilment of God's will as the banquet of the heavenly kingdom. It had been such a focal point that it became a crucial link between that pre-Easter fellowship of Jesus and his disciples, and the fellowship of the later resurrection community, the Christian Church. Time and again it was the eucharist which focused for our Parables in Action group the intimate relationship between Jesus and his servants throughout the ages. It was a source of great joy on several occasions when our parish eucharist specifically centred upon the experiences and discoveries of the group. So often this sacrament enacted for us what we were trying to express in other ways by serving action and by reflective word. We meditated upon the fact that all were freely invited to Christ's table, the lame, sinners and publicans alike, and this open invitation to liberated sharing had been an abrasive affront to the exclusiveness and 'piety' of the then prevailing understandings of human relationships one with another and with God. So Jesus' table was an active symbol of the defeat of those powers which would separate, categorise and penalise. When that table-fellowship had been further overlaid with the sacramental significance of the cross at the Last Supper, then the eucharistic fellowship displayed and symbolised in this great sacrament, the self-sacrifice necessary for that dethroning of all Power and Empire. But the history of the eucharist epitomises the Church's reluctance to stay true to this sacrificial element in the gospel and by the middle ages the mass had been blurred by symbols of domination and exclusivity so that the breaking of the bread and the pouring out of the wine had been all but obscured. The eucharist was perverted and used to contribute to the subjection of so many as it was hawked across the globe by imperialist Europe. Priests had interpreted the mass as a directive to submission and obedience to the ruling authorities, and its sacramental power as a prefiguration of the sharing forgiveness of the Kingdom was all but forgotten.(15)

But despite this attempt on the part of the powers to subjugate the institutional eucharist to their will, the authentic Christian community can still find in sacramental table-fellowship the same power to liberate and save as it had when Jesus presided during his earthly ministry. It becomes again part of the alternative life which the powers of evil cannot understand; it remains a holy mystery. The eucharist became more and more central to our spiritual life at St. Chad's but we were constantly trying to find ways to make our parish communion services as inclusive and as liberative as possible, in response to what we had been learning. In this, as in so many other ways, the new things we had been discovering through our project were forever being fed into the ongoing life of the wider church congregation. And the eucharist in its turn had taught us that despite all the odds, the Kingdom was amongst us and we could participate in it thankfully. The eucharist became a constant reference point for us to which we repeatedly returned to find solidarity with Jesus, the prime witness to our faith in the transcendent in the midst. In it we could see Jesus cutting away all the dominating structural barriers, as black shared with white, male with female, young with old. It was for us a model of the new society of total self-sharing which will never let us be content with injustice or domination.

(ii) The Prophetic Word

We could clearly perceive that our attitudes had been greatly influenced by our project but we were also aware that our language had been changing too. Many of the prejudicial sentiments which we tended to share with the wider society were not even noticed initially but, as our work progressed, as our experience and reflection bore fruit, so we perceived that we were increasingly sensitive to prejudicial remarks or terminology. It seemed that the English language itself was one of those structures which had to be made to conform to the demands of the Gospel too, and when we heard or used prejudicial phrases such as 'problem families', 'non-white', 'lower-class', 'client' or 'the nature of man', we began to wince discernably.

'It's a bit like the Old Testament prophets who had to proclaim new words from the Lord', said John. 'At least that's how it feels. The old words just won't do any more because now we know something about oppression that we didn't know before.'

So, to the struggle to change our old perceptions into Gospel orientated perceptions, came the prophetic resource of new words. We have grown up with our language, our mother tongue, and have learnt to think our simplest and our most penetrating thoughts using its images. It has thereby won for itself a subtle but profound authority deep in our psyches and we don't relinquish one 'if' or 'but' of it without some anguish. How painful a revelation it is then when we find out that even the English language is a fallen structure! What last-ditch battles we are prepared to fight before we allow the language to be changed to conform to the Gospel mandates! What contemptuous looks you'll get if you even enquire as to whether the language of our liturgies might be saved from its sexist exclusivity. To change our language to conform more to the Gospel of Christ is to engage in the proclamation of the Word of God over against the power of English words. We had learnt how hard it was and yet how powerful a tool it could prove in the struggle with the powers. We ourselves never found it easy to tear ourselves away from exclusive religious language and the discerning reader will still have noted my own reluctance and insensitivities in these chapters about such words as 'Kingdom', 'Father' and 'Sons'.

We have mentioned the eucharistic sacrament, we have mentioned the prophetic new word, but from amongst the great treasure-house of resources at the disposal of the Christian Community we must of course finally return to that with which this project began, the activity of Parables.

(iii) Parables in Action

We had always hoped that our total project, of Community Advice Centre and Parables in Action Group, would in some way become itself an acted parable and a sacramental action. In view of all that had happened, could this now be said to be at all true?

We had looked carefully at the community and society around us, as Jesus had done, and we had worked hard on discovering God's will and purpose within all that we had experienced. We had tried to keep these two aspects of the project constantly interrelating, but now, after so long, we attempted to evaluate what had happened. This evaluation was undertaken carefully and systematically. We sent round questionnaires to all sorts of local people and invited outside specialists in to view and criticise the project – we were keen to give those inside and outside the Church an opportunity to tell us honestly what they thought. By this time the Community Advice Centre had itself been operating for nearly two years and so we were able to look back to the hopes we had had when we had started out, to see if we had accomplished our aims. In those early days, you will remember, we had spelt out four goals for ourselves and against each we had tried to determine by what criteria we would assess ourselves after two years of operation. That time had now come and so the group spent a whole Saturday together to go through carefully all the data and questionnaire responses to see if our Parable in Action had really borne fruit. Above all, we wanted to know if the project had affected people's perceptions and helped to direct attention and energies towards the liberating Gospel of Jesus.

There was no doubt that those who were engaged in the project at every level were registering an extraordinary sense of empowerment. 'It's enabled me to do things I never thought I could. If you'd have asked me two years ago if I could have been of any help to people with real problems like this, I would have been too shy to answer, let alone do anything.'

'I feel just like that paralysed man Jesus healed', said another respondent. 'I had always relied on others before, but now I can rely on the strength God seems to have given

me.' There were those who were surprised to see themselves
actually doing things, taking responsibilities and initiatives;
there were others who spoke of an inner healing and grace.
One person went so far as to record, 'I feel I've turned from
dying to life!'

Whilst I as vicar of the parish had learnt a great deal about
the arts of listening and serving, it was clear that many of
those within the project had become tremendously articulate
human beings, more able to witness in word and deed to
their faith. They had indeed been so invigorated by their
experience in the project that they were keen to share their
learning with as wide an audience as possible. Visitors who
had come to the Centre told us that they felt they too had
grown in confidence in themselves and in faith in others.
They no longer felt so isolated and were less inclined to
attach unnecessary blame to themselves for their plight.
Attendance at the Centre was steadily growing and local
people were using the amenity easily and naturally. The
advising team had grown in numbers and confidence too
under Madeleine's and Alan's superb leadership. A new
radical awareness had set in at the project itself and new
insights were expressed at many levels. Regularly it was said,
'we can now see more clearly that helping people through a
problem, however important it is to do that, doesn't necessarily do anything to take away the root cause of the problem.
You have to change society to do that, and that takes a lot
of hope and faith.' There seemed to be a new hope and
vigour around at St. Chad's and a stirring conviction that
despite all the powerlessness, there were enough 'Signs of
the Kingdom' to be seen, that people said with confidence
and resilience, 'Jesus is Lord', 'Good *can* Win!'

We were only too aware of many shortcomings in ourselves
and in our project and we did not want to pat ourselves on
the back but we had a conviction that we had been sharing
in a Parable in Action. In that we now had a vehicle with
which to confront the powers, and within it were opportunities to treat the powers as the servants of the suffering, even
where these powers still tried to claim dominating authority,
then our Community Advice Centre was a parable of the
Kingdom's action. In that our Parables in Action group gave

us opportunity to reflect on the reversals which God was enacting, then here too the project was parabolic. In that we were now in much closer fellowship from day to day with the suffering of our community, and our role was specifically a serving one, then the project was giving us a glimpse of Kingdom activity in our midst. 'It is only a glimpse since the Kingdom itself has, as we've seen, much wider cosmic significance; but now at least we are engaged in a way that never would have been possible before.'

The Parables in Action group had always been aware of its important goal to be of service to the Church too and to share its experience and learning as much as it could. To this end, they wrote a small workbook called *St. Chad's Read and Think Book* which took the reader step by step through the story of the project and explained some of the theological insights that had emerged. At the same time as the workbook was being circulated, articles about our learning appeared in the parish magazine, *Chad*. At the same time, a second great worship service of celebration took place which had been devised by the group so that the congregation could share something of what the group had experienced of the power of powerlessness. Constantly the influence of the group's actions and reflections were felt around the parish and within the daily life of St. Chad's Church itself as it sought at every level to be more and more the servant of the community. The local community itself could sense it too and it was becoming clear that local people looked upon the church as a friendly landmark in an area with many difficulties and as a plain witness to the powerful self-giving of Jesus.

I asked: 'How shall we compare the Kingdom of God activity? – Could we compare it to what we've seen in our little project?' There was a long silence while we thought of all its limitations and all the things that we knew were still wrong with it and with us, but after a moment of hesitation, Colin leaned forward in his chair and with conviction whispered, 'Yes, it's coming.'

C. Personal afterthoughts

We all wish no doubt that we had been granted the gift of 'knowing then what we know now'. With hindsight, many of us who were engaged in the Community Advice Centre and in the Parables in Action group would have gone about things very differently. There were many important, indeed crucial avenues which we did not explore in our theological investigations and there was always the question of whether one should range broadly across many issues or focus heavily upon just a few. Perhaps one is bound to end up with only a partial view whichever approach one plumps for. It might have been good to look more intently at the issues of racism, sexism, housing or health, but as it was, many of those participating began to make some of those connections for themselves.

A major fault, it seems to me, was that our theological reflection relied far too much on verbal articulation and much more could have been accomplished had we explored earlier more non-verbal ways into our theologising. The remarkable thing is that over the years so many of the participants unexpectedly did become verbally articulate and quite powerfully so.

One of my strongest misgivings about the project will, I fancy, always be to do with the fact that the people in the Parables in Action group were not themselves those who were in really abject powerlessness. We constantly ran the risk of patronising the powerless. The group was assuredly representative of the community and quite rightly therefore was essentially working-class but none of us were really at the extreme margins of our society. There was an important factor however which somewhat reduced this distance from those in most need. We experienced throughout the project the most extraordinary run of illness and grief. Jim was one of our number who, at an early stage in the project, was found to be suffering from leukemia and died soon after. Fred, our churchwarden who had been thoroughly committed to the project, died suddenly and without any prior warning of ill-health. Soon after that, Emily died of cancer and her husband Jack suffered a severe stroke, but remained in the group despite his paralysis. And so it went on, to the extent that our personal experiences of powerlessness and sorrow at times felt almost overwhelming. We loved each one of these folk so dearly and yet it was their loss, I am sure, which inspired an even warmer atmosphere of tenderness and forthright compassion all around the project, and in a sense saved us from ourselves. There was an intense longing to learn from the powerless, as well as to be of service to them. We tried to make our own, the story from the life of Vincent de Paul. He was the Father Confessor to a house of French nuns, the Sisters of Charity, who spent their whole lives in the service of the very poor – those who were looked down upon by most of society. One day, the nuns came to Vincent and asked him, 'Father, teach us to pray in preparation for our work of mercy to these people.' He simply replied, 'Pray that they may forgive you.'(16)

Despite the many limitations of the project, I hope that it did go some little way towards proving that it is important that a liberative theology be worked out here in Britain. At St. Chad's, we only took one small illustrative bite at that cherry and many may feel that not much that is new has been achieved, But I sense that the most significant factor in the whole endeavour is that at St. Chad's 'the people of God' discovered theology as a felt experience and made it for themselves. The type of theology which was produced, is I believe in itself worthy of note too. As our group went deeper and deeper into the questions of theodicy and power and powerlessness, so it built for itself a practical understanding or 'working theology' to live by. It is possible to prod holes in the logic and theoretical streamlining of the arguments but in terms of its Christian 'usability' I would hazard to say that it's pretty robust. Theologians use the words 'orthodoxy' and 'orthopraxis' to distinguish between theologies which are valid by virtue of their theoretical content or their practical faithfulness, but the Parables in Action group seem to me to have passed both tests reasonably well simply by remaining true to their conviction that their Lord was already in the world of need, calling them to mission alongside him.

I personally must remain very thankful for the project for it gave me a new vision of priesthood set within the body of

God's Church. I experienced the great rewards of the self-
discipline of listening and enabling, and learnt the bitter
lesson that the dominating priest disables the Spirit in the
community. My role became clearer week by week as I
serviced the group, dropped in the awkward questions or
supported and affirmed the project members when they felt
that they were not making headway. As the laity became
stronger, so they called upon me only for the more specialist
tasks and resources and did not expect me to be a 'Jack of
all trades and master of none'. As I shared my vulnerability
with them, so they enabled me by their prayers, insights and
strengths, to play my rightful part with courage and vigour.
They helped me to discern my gifts, my strengths and weaknesses and were instrumental in helping me to focus even
more sharply the nature of my priestly vocation. The
important role I had learnt to play within the groups was that
of the facilitator who constantly encouraged each member to
have faith in their self and in the value of their contribution.
My task, especially in the early stages, had been to help
members to express what they were trying to say. I sensed
that it was important that I had been well schooled myself
in making the faith-life connections so as to encourage others
to do the same. The more I got into the project the clearer
it became that to do theology at this level demands more
honest 'street credibility' than sophisticated 'restaurant presence'! In that, I had been helped by training in the USA
where I had been encouraged to own my own very working-
class roots, and by my long association with the Revd Dr.
John Vincent who was always around the project to advise
and to discuss theological matters with. In addition to all
this, as a participant the overall experience encouraged me
to further my research into the important structures of Class
in Britain and how that basic factor of our national life relates
to our task as the Church in mission.[17]

During the process of the project, I learnt too that the
theologian is there to work with the raw material and the
situations which God gives. If dwindling numbers had been
our church's problem, then that would have been our Gospel
starting-point. If we had got ourselves stuck during the
project then we would have had to work on a theology of

'stuckness'. We eventually found that theologising had found its way into our life blood so that we were making faith-life connections everywhere we looked. We could not think about the church mums-and-toddlers club or the youth club or the outreach committee, or even the Church Council, without checking our every move against the wisdom and mandates of the Gospel. We got into the habit of being constantly on the lookout for God's Unexpected and in that regard we were all astonished by the way that indigenous leaders and gifted local people kept popping up in this so-called deprived area, once we had learnt to look with new understanding.

And while I was learning so much, other members of the group were developing in new ways too. A couple of the members were stimulated to set up discussion groups and work groups of their own. Some became more involved in community action, others concerned themselves with worship and evangelism, and I have recently learnt that one of the black members of the group is now realising that she might have to respond to a call to some sort of ordained ministry in the Church. But perhaps it is best to let the now so articulate words of Sue, another member, speak for themselves:

'I think I speak for all of us when I say that arising out of this project has come a much closer commitment to this particular patch of the inner city area, a much more practical grasp of its needs, and an awareness of living within a caring, sharing community. Dare I mention a certain feeling of affection for a rather unlovely place – and that would never have happened without this project. Also, and most important of all, we have learnt that theology is something that can be done by quite ordinary people. We have plenty of evidence, in the tapes of all the meetings, of ordinary people making quite extra-ordinary insights into the nature of God, the Ministry of the Church, and Signs of the Kingdom. Arguments about the Beast, Powers and Principalities, Parables, all spilled over into other group meetings and off-the-cuff discussions in the school playground as we mums waited for our kids to come out of school.

We've been helped to discover that theology is not an activity undertaken a hundred years ago, by remote clergymen writing dusty old sermons; it's something that can be done today. It's a practical exercise that involves action, like the setting up of an Advice Centre or whatever, and reflection upon that action. We have experienced a feeling of growing self-confidence in ourselves as theologians. Theology is too important to be left to the ministers of the Church – but that's a bit cheeky to say that!'

To make this book manageable, I have had to omit descriptions of whole areas and episodes such as the parties, the outings, the arguments and mistakes, the many dead-ends that we ventured up in our explorations, and I have recorded only the more significant events and discoveries. The Community Advice Centre continues, under Madeleine's leadership, to gain more experience to be reflected upon and only recently celebrated its sixth anniversary. Some of us, myself included, have moved on to fresh challenges elsewhere. But I hope nevertheless that this book has offered at least a flavour of something of our experience as we sought together under the shadow of Spaghetti Junction to find a vibrant and passionate theology to live by. My one hope is that our story may inspire others to go further.

Notes

Chapter One

1. The ways in which the status quo is maintained through the systems of our society have been thoroughly described and analysed by the Critical School of sociology. The anthology edited by Paul Connerton entitled *Critical Sociology* (Penguin, 1976) is a fine introduction to the depth of their work. Cf. also Marcuse, *One Dimensional Man*, (Beacon Press, 1964). p. 12ff.

2. The A.C.U.P.A. report, *Faith in the City* (Church House Publishing, 1985) has amassed statistical evidence which has never been questioned, even by its harshest critics, of how those living in the so-called Urban Priority Areas are disadvantaged at every turn. The figures are bleak and demand response. Constant statistical updating on the international scene can be found in the journal *The New Internationalist* (available from 120 Lavender Ave. Mitcham Surrey), which constantly challenges cosiness with harsh facts.

3. Mark 1:14–15 (New Jerusalem Bible)

4. For a readable survey and evaluation of Liberation Theology see *Revolutionary Theology Comes of Age* by J. Miguez Bonino (SPCK, 1975). Hear Nicaraguan Christians doing liberation Bible study in *Love in Practice – The Gospel in Solentiname* by Ernesto Cardinal (Search Press, 1977).

5. Ian Fraser, *Reinventing Theology as the People's Work* (USPG. London undated), and in *Theology by the People* ed. S. Amirtham & J. Pobee (WCC, 1986)

6. See *Can these Dry Bones Live?*, Frances Young (SCM Press, 1982) and cf. the work of Gramsci in the political sphere, where he argues in parallel manner that the political theorist is more dangerous than useful if allowed to become separated from the 'masses'. e.g. *Letters from Prison* transl. L. Lawner (Quartet Books, 1973)

7. Note for example the different thrusts represented in the contributions made from a variety of cultures in the recent *Theology by the People* (WCC 1986)

8. See for example *The Liberation of Theology* by J. L. Segundo (Gill & Macmillan, 1977) and the first and final sections of *Theology in the Making* ed. Ruth Musgrave (NACCCAN, Birmingham 1982)

9. See the continuing work and publications from the Urban Theology Unit in Sheffield; the research papers from St. Peter's Saltley Trust, Birmingham; the stories and publications of the Evangelical Coalition for Urban Mission, London. Also the valuable collection in *Agenda for Prophets* eds. Ambler & Haslam (Bowerdean, 1980)

Chapter Two

1. This title indicates how distinct Birmingham's history has been as compared with, say, Manchester or Sheffield whose large-scale concerns were dominant factors in the early industrial period. This is attested in early research – e.g. John Morley's *Life of Richard Cobden* (Chapman & Hall, 1881) See also my paper on 'The Decaying Cities of Britain' in *St George's House Windsor, Annual Review 1984*.

2. Even as late as 1976 the National Consultative Committee for Local Ecumenical Projects had only registered 104 Anglican/Methodist projects. The unity agreement at St Chad's was legally recognised under the Sharing of Church Buildings Act 1969 and the parish designated by the Birmingham Regional Sponsoring Body as an 'Area of Ecumenical Experiment'. Only later did the more acceptable title of 'Local Ecumenical Project' gain recognition thus indicating the provisional nature of denominationalism and challenging the false understanding of ecumenism as 'experimental'. Cf. the *Draft of the Ecumenical Relations Measure and Canons Study Guide* (B.M.U., General Synod of the C of E, 1985). A handbook on the subject of Local Ecumenical Projects is available from CCLEPE (Consultative Committee for Local Ecumenical Projects in England), care of the British Council of Churches, London.

3. The Kingsbury Road Community Centre was established in 1976, at a disused college annex, after pressure from the church, political parties and local welfare agencies. The author chaired the Centre Management Committee from its inception thus cementing the link between Church and Centre.

4. J. Jeremias opens his authoritative book, *The Parables of Jesus*

(SCM Press, 1972) with the statement, 'The student of the parables of Jesus, as they have been transmitted to us in the first three Gospels, may be confident that he stands upon a particularly firm historical foundation'.

5. See the work of Paulo Freire, esp. *Education for Critical Consciousness* (Sheed & Ward, 1974) pp 150 – 155 and *Pedagogy of the Oppressed* (Penguin, 1972). Cf. the philosophical work of Adorno as described in Connerton's *Critical Sociology*.

6. See *The Act of Creation*, Arthur Koestler (Hutchinson, London 1964) p111ff,pp 121–4.

7. Robert Holman's *Power for the Powerless: The Role of Community Action*, (BCC, London 1972) p15.

8. Freire in his *Pedagogy of the Oppressed* (Penguin, 1972) uses the term 'dialogical education' for this style of educational process. See also Brian Wren's *Education for Justice* (SCM Press, 1977) and the scholarly survey of the philosophy underpinning this style by Martin Jay, *The Dialectical Imagination* (Heinemann, 1973). John Hull has written a practical theology of Christian education which is likely to become a classic, entitled *What Prevents Christian Adults from Learning?* (SCM Press, 1985)

9. The notion of the 'alternative within' is drawn from Hegel's philosophy and is taken up once more to great effect by Marcuse. See for example his *One Dimensional Man* (Beacon Press, 1964) p63ff, and *Negations. Essays in Critical Theory*. (Penguin, Allen Lane, 1968)

10. For example, witness the work of Norman K. Gottwald, *The Tribes of Yahweh* (SCM Press, 1979) where evidence is documented to indicate, amongst other things, the way in which the original story of liberation movements in Palestine was overlaid with material which changes the perspective to that of the later more conservative editors.

11. Deut.26:5 (RSV)

12. The Domesday entry recorded in Hingeley's *Erdington since the Conquest* (1900. Birmingham City Library ref. 155285) p8, speaks of a place of great potential – 'a manor worth thirty shillings, fourteen families, a mill, about thirty acres of arable land and a wood'.

13. See the research work of Renate and John Wilkinson in *Inheritors Together* (Theology & Racism 2 Race, Pluralism and Community Group, Board of Social Responsibility of the General Synod of the CofE, 1985) Also *Anglicans and Racism: The Balsall Heath Consultation 1986* (from the same publisher, 1986)

14. The *Faith in the City* report suggests that a Parish Audit be

undertaken. This notion is drawn from the British pioneering work of Urban Theology Unit and Urban Ministry Project. A number of useful guides to this process have since become available: *Towards Local Social Analysis* (CAP, 27 Blackfriars Rd. Salford); *Discovering the Poor: a kit for local groups* (U.T.U., 210 Abbeyfield Rd, Sheffield); *Mission Audit* BMU (C10 Publishing, 1984). Also, see the continuing publications of the Evangelical Urban Training Project and the Grove Booklets; and Diocese of Birmingham, *Parish Response Proposals*.

15. The 'small area census' statistics were available of course, plus much more valuable information once the local Planning Department of the City Council understood our needs. The Diocese of Birmingham is currently working on a series of visual display systems so that detailed statistics in digestible form can be available to all parishes from the Diocesan centre.

Chapter Three

1. Luke 16:1–8
2. Matt. 25:14–30
3. John Vincent is the Director of the Urban Theology Unit in Sheffield who throughout this project acted as a personal supervisor to me. He also worked with the Revd Dr. Dick Snyder in overseeing my doctoral research which underpinned and derived from much of the work of the Parables in Action project. See my *In the Face of Domination* (Unpublished thesis, 1982)
4. See for example *Jesus in Bad Company* by Adolf Holl, (Collins, 1972), *Radical Discipleship*, J. Sugden (Marshalls, 1983); *Jesus's Audience* J. D. M. Derrett (D.L.T., 1973) and of course *Jerusalem in the Time of Jesus*, by Jeremias (S.C.M. Press, 1969)
5. Luke 21:1–4
6. Mark 10:13–16
7. Luke 10:29–37
8. Luke 10:25–28
9. The two 'Commandments of Jesus' are drawn from Deuteronomy 6:5 and Leviticus 19:18 in accordance with common rabbinic practice.
10. See for example *The Analogical Imagination* by David Tracey (S.C.M. Press, 1981) and the more readable *Education for Justice* by Brian Wren (S.C.M. Press, 1977)
11. We record thanks to the National Association of Citizens' Advice Bureaux and especially to the Birmingham Central Office for their gracious advice and cooperation throughout the project.

12. Cf. Ivan Illich, *Disabling Professions* (Open Forum, Marion Boyars Ltd. 1977)
13. *Gilding the Ghetto – the State of the Poverty Experiments*, Inter-Project Editorial Team (Community Development Project, 1977) tells the story of the C.D.P.'s, their rise and demise.

Chapter Four

1. Thomas Kuhn, *The Structure of Scientific Revolutions'* (University of Chicago Press, 1962) esp. p 110ff.
2. J. Jeremias, *The Parables of Jesus*, study edition pp 101–102.
3. 2 Samuel 12:1–15
4. Adolf Jülicher, *Die Gleichnisreden Jesu* (J. C. B. Mohr, Siebech 1888/9)
5. Luke 16:1–8
6. C. H. Dodd, *The Parables of the Kingdom* (Fontana revised edition, 1961)
7. Psalm 146:7–10 (Jerusalem Bible)
8. Cf. R. Schnackenburg, *God's Rule & Kingdom* (Herder & Herder, 1963)
9. Luke 11:20 (RSV) and see Norman Perrin, *Rediscovering the Teaching of Jesus* (SCM Press, 1967) p.67 where a detailed study of this proclamation is set out with reference to the Qumran material.
10. Eg. Isaiah 25:6–8, and the many references to the Passover Meal. Also see the *Dictionary of New Testament Theology*, ed. C. Brown (Paternoster Press, 1976) Vol 2, pp.520ff
11. Luke 8:43–48
12. Luke 5:12–14
13. Mark 7:24–30
14. Mark 2:23–28
15. Mark 14:17–31
16. Mark 4:12
17. See the superb study entitled, *Alienation* by Bertell Ollman (Cambridge University Press, Second Edition 1976). The play-wright Bertolt Brecht believed that the proper task of theatre was to produce what he called the 'estrangement effect' in the audience by which they would be made to feel at odds with the way things are so that things could be properly criticised. The philosopher Adorno said much the same thing about French surrealist art. Brecht, *Schriften zum Theater* (Suhrkamp, 1957). Adorno, *Noten zur Literatur* (Suhrkamp, 1958)
18. Cf. E. Linnemann *Parables of Jesus: Introduction and Exposition*, trans. J. Sturdy (S.P.C.K., 1966)

19. Luke 4:16–22

20. S. Kierkegaard, *The Point of View* (Oxford University Press, 1950) p25. Cf. also *Hamlet*, Act II, Scene 2 – 'The play's the thing/ wherein I'll catch the conscience of the King.'

21. Mark 3:27 (RSV) The same point is made in the fascinating little book by Robert Short entitled *The Parables of Peanuts* (Harper & Row, 1968)

22. The idea was culled from a session designed around 'management by objectives' techniques by the Urban Theology Unit, Sheffield.

Chapter Five

1. It is difficult to remain objective about the staff of the DHSS and other state agencies when you have borne insult and abuse from some of their number. Most inner city clergy such as myself, would probably have stories too many to number. I think that it must be said however that the majority of our local workers were operating reasonably well considering the severe limitations upon them.

2. An interesting discussion of the dilemma is to be found in *In and Against the State*, by the London Edinburgh Weekend Return Group (Pluto Press, 1980)

3. Ralph McTell, *Streets of London* (Essex Music International Ltd., 1968 & 72)

4. Detailed statistics are to be found in Renate Wilkinson's article 'A Chance to Change' in *Inheritors Together* p.23.

5. Sue held in great affection the poem by John Milton, *On His Blindness*, which can be found in many anthologies of English Poetry. She was particularly struck by the final line, 'They also serve who only stand and wait.'

6. Matt.15:21–28 & Mark 7: 24–30. The group used the Jerusalem Bible translation.

7. The major thrust of the *Faith in the City* report is upon the need for the church and its people to listen to the marginalised.

8. To be found in the book by Gladys Elder, OAP, entitled *The Alienated – Growing Old Today*, (Writers and Readers Publishing Cooperative, 1977) pp 7–9.

9. Luke 9:46–48. Cf. Luke 18:15–17

10. Paul Tillich, *The Shaking of the Foundations* (SCM Press, 1949) Chapter 8.

11. Psalm 130:5–8, (Jerusalem Bible)

12. Luke 2:29–32

13. Matthew 4:1–11: Luke 4:1–13; and the very short allusion in Mark 1: 12–13

14. Luke 4:4 (New Jerusalem Bible) quoted from Deut.8:3

15. There are constant references to the amazement of the crowds in the synoptic tradition, as evidenced clearly in Mark's account e.g. Mark 5:41; 5:20,42; 8:37

16. A fascinating challenge on this principle is presented by George W. Weber in *Today's Church: a Community of Exiles and Pilgrims* (Abingdon, 1979) p 30ff.

17. John 5:1–18

18. The subsequent events in the story and Jesus' words to the cured man in private about his sin (v14) indicate that the group's interpretation of the passage warrants careful consideration.

Chapter Six

1. An estimated nine million people are under arms at present in the Warsaw Pact and NATO countries alone. Half a million scientists are said to be working on the development of new weapons.

2. Senate hearings in the United States have revealed something of the degree to which companies such as I. T. T. have dictated American home and international policy. See for example Anthony Sampson, *Sovereign State: The Secret History of I. T. T.* (Hodder & Stoughton, 1973)

3. *The New Internationalist* magazine is available from 120 Lavender Ave. Mitcham, Surrey.

4. The centripetal nature of economic power is discussed in the classic study by Berle and Means, *The Modern Corporation and Private Property* (Macmillan, 1940).

5. The starry-eyed pictures painted by Richard Hoggart and others in the 1950s about British working class life must not be allowed to cloud our understanding of what is now happening. The boom and rehousing programmes of the 60's have changed working-class life out of all recognition.

6. Lord Acton *Historical Essays and Studies*, Ed. J. Figgis & R. V. Laurence (Macmillan, 1907)

7. See M. Heidegger *Being and Time* (Harper and Row, 1962) and cf. Alfred Adler *Religion und Individual Psychologie*, with E. Jahn (Wien u. Leipzig 1933) p58 where he argues that 'The striving of every individual is directed towards achievement, not towards power', death being the denial of this basic striving. cf. *The Practice and Theory of Individual Psychology*, Adler (Routledge and Kegan Paul Ltd., 1964), esp. the first chapter.

8. Cf. Romans 7:15 'I do not understand my own behaviour; I do not act as I mean to, but I do the thing I hate.' (New Jerusalem Bible)

9. Reinhold Niebuhr, *Moral Man & Immoral Society* (SCM Press, 1963) pp xi – xii

10. John Howard Yoder, *The Politics of Jesus* (W. D. Eerdmans Publishing Co., 1972) p 190.

11. Colossians 1:16–17 (NEB) The Authorised Version of King James translated 'authorities and powers' as 'principalities and powers' and this latter phrase has been used ever since in relation to this and related verses as a matter of tradition. It may be noted that some scholars still maintain that the Colossian letter was not written by St. Paul. I believe that more recent scholarship suggests that it was, but this would not in any case detract from the importance of the point being made in the text.

12. For evidence of the correctness of this understanding of the language see for example H. Berkhof's *Christ and the Powers* (Herald Press, 1962); G. B. Caird's *Principalities and Powers* (Clarendon, 1956); Martin Hengel's, *Christ and Power* (Christian Journals Ltd. 1977); A. van den Heuvel's, *These Rebellious Powers* (SCM Press, 1966)

13. Colossians 1:16–17 & 2:20ff. Cf Galatians 4:3

14. Romans 8:38

15. Romans 7:12 (& cf. Galatians 4:5)

16. Romans 1:18 ff (and cf. the language of Ephesians 2:1–3)

17. Cf. *Christ and Culture* by H. Richard Niebuhr (Harper, 1951)

18. For a full discussion of the historical symbolism see John Court's *Myth and History in the Book of Revelation* (SPCK, 1979) and John Sweet's *Revelation* (SCM Press, 1979)

19. Ephesians 6:12 (NEB)

20. *In and Against the State* by the London Edinburgh Weekend Return Group.

21. The group was much intrigued by the poem by Brecht on this subject entitled 'A Bed for the Night' in *Bertold Brecht: Poems 1913–1956*, J Willett (Eyre Methuen Ltd.,1981)

22. Cf. T. Adorno, *Sociology and Psychology* (New Left Review, 46, Nov-Dec 1967 & 47, Jan-Feb 1968)

23. See *Gilding the Ghetto. The State of the Poverty Experiments*

24. See *In and Against the State* pp 34 ff.

25. Mary W. Shelley, *Frankenstein: a Modern Prometheus* (Dent & Sons Ltd, 1963) originally published anonymously in 1818.

26. Romans 8:38–39; Galatians 4:3.

27. Berkhof notes that 'The German people have been especially

prepared, both by character and by most recent history for a new understanding of the "Powers".' in *Christ and the Powers* (Herald Press, 1962 from the original Dutch 1953) p.15

Chapter Seven

1. We need only cite the example of the use of story amongst the people of Northern Ireland at present to realise that sometimes hard analysis is better (although perhaps less potent) than reliance on folk memories.

2. Augustine, *The Confessions of Augustine* VII.3. (Penguin,1961) p.136 and see his further reflections in VII,12,13 and 16, pp.148–150.

3. St. Irenaeus, *Against Heresies*.V.vi.I, and see John Lawson's *The Biblical Theology of St Irenaeus* (Epworth,1948)

4. See the thorough exposition and discussion of the Augustinian and Irenaean arguments in John Hick's *Evil and the God of Love* (Macmillan, 3rd Edition, 1985)

5. John Keats' letter to his brother and sister dated April 1819. He continues 'Do you not see how necessary a World of Pains and Troubles is to school an Intelligence and make it a Soul?' *The letters of John Keats* ed. M. B. Forman (Oxford University Press, 4th Edition 1952)

6. 2 Corinthians 12:9–10 (NEB)

7. Luke 22:66 – 23:1 This was most probably a preliminary hearing rather than a proper trial – cf. H. Danby, 'The Bearing of the Rabbinical Code on the Jewish Trial Narratives in the Gospels' in *Journal of Theological Studies* xxi pp 51f.

8. Luke 23:1–25

9. Pilate's actions several times provoked riots and in 36 A.D. he was recalled to Rome to account for disorder in Samaria. Eusebius says he committed suicide.

10. e.g. Mark 2:10

11. e.g. Mark 1:31–34; 4:41

12. e.g. Mark 1:24; 5:7

13. Philippians 2:6–11. 'Song of Christ's Glory', *Alternative Service Book 1980* (CofE) p 67

14. Vincent Taylor, *The Gospel According to St. Mark* (Macmillan, 1963) p589

15. Matthew 27:32–56

16. Matthew 27:45, 51–53

17. Yoder, *The Politics of Jesus* p.148

18. On Pauline authorship of Colossians see Chapter 6, footnote 11

19. Colossians 2:15 (NEB)

20. I have taken this passage to refer to a change in perception, not a dissolution of the structures *per se*. This is because the verb *apekduomai* is used of 'casting off garments' rather than of disgarding weaponry. Those like Berkhof and Ronald Sider who tend to follow the latter reading must explain why they feel the verb must change its meaning on this occasion. See Arndt & Gingrich *A Greek-English Lexicon of the New Testament and other Early Christian Literature* (Cambridge University Press, 4th Edition 1957)

21. Cf. the classic *Love's Endeavour, Love's Expense* by W. H. Vanstone (Darton, Longman and Todd, 1977)

Chapter Eight

1. Ephesians 1:20–21. (NEB)

2. Ronald Sider, *Christ and Violence* (Lion Publishing, 1980) p51

3. Sermon preached by Martin Luther King Jnr., Washington, August 1963

4. Romans 13:1–7

5. 2 Corinthians 5:17

6. I Corinthians 4:13 (NEB)

7. Cf. John 3:14; 12:32; 17:1

8. John 19:30 (NEB)

9. J. Stevenson (ed), *A New Eusebius* (SPCK, 1963) p42

10. Text in Knopf-Krüger, *Ausgewählte Märtyrerakten* (Mohr, 1965) pp 93–94

11. See 'The Lamb's War' by the early Quaker James Nayler, 1658, to be found in *Early Quaker Writings 1650–1700*, ed. Hugh Barbour and Arthur O. Roberts (Eerdmans, 1973)

12. See Daniel Berrigan's chapter on 'Sanity in the face of the Beast' in *Seeds of Liberation*. ed. Alistair Kee (SCM Press, 1973)

13. Matthew 28:18–20

14. Helmut Gollwitzer, 'Die Revolution des Reiches Gottes und die Gesellschaft' in *Diskussion zur 'Theologie der Revolution'* ed. Feil and Weth. (Kaiser & Matthias Grünewald, 1969)

15. See Tissa Balasuriya, *The Eucharist and Human Liberation* (SCM Press, 1977) where this case is strongly argued.

16. See *The World of Monsieur Vincent*, by M. Purcell (Harvill Press, 1963)

17. See my *In the Face of Domination* unpublished thesis 1982, which includes a study of class in British Society.

If you wish to receive *regular information* about *new books*, please send your name and address to:

London Bible Warehouse
PO Box 123
Basingstoke
Hants RG23 7NL

Name...

Address...

....

....

....

I am especially interested in:
- ☐ Biographies
- ☐ Fiction
- ☐ Christian living
- ☐ Issue related books
- ☐ Academic books
- ☐ Bible study aids
- ☐ Children's books
- ☐ Music
- ☐ Other subjects